Hermeneutics

Bernard L. Ramm and Others

BAKER BOOK HOUSE
Grand Rapids, Michigan

ISBN: 0-8010-7605-6
First Printing, March 1971
Second Printing, August 1972
Third Printing, August 1974
Fourth Printing, February 1976
Fifth Printing, November 1977

The contents of this book originally appeared as Section 3 of *Baker's Dictionary of Practical Theology,* edited by Ralph G. Turnbull, © 1967 by Baker Book House Company.

Contents

1

Biblical Interpretation

1. INTRODUCTION

The Protestant ministry is based upon the Word of God as expressed in the inspired canonical literature and as perpetuated in preaching. Whereas in Roman Catholicism the Christian servant is a priest whose primary function is sacramental, in Protestantism the Christian servant is a minister whose central function is the ministry of the Word of God. Although the Christian ministry is manifold and ought not to be seen exclusively as preaching, without doubt it reaches its fullest expression in the preaching of the Word of God.

If this is the nature of the Protestant ministry it follows that one of the most important considerations of the Christian ministry must be the right use of the Word of God. Paul tells Timothy that he is to handle rightly the word of truth (II Tim. 2:15. Greek: *orthotomeō*, to cut a straight line, to guide the word of truth along a straight line). A cardinal sin of false ministers is that they abuse (*kapēleuō*, to be huckster, to adulterate) the Word of God (II Cor. 2:17). The main concern in the right use of the Word of God is its proper interpretation. Whether preaching is textual or topical or expository it rests ultimately upon the minister's interpretation of the Word of God. That theological discipline which takes as its goal the proper interpretation of Scripture is hermeneutics. A solid hermeneutics is the root of all good exegesis and exegesis is the foundation of all truly Biblical preaching. Therefore a sound hermeneutics is an absolute *desideratum* for the minister of the Word of God.

Although traditionally hermeneutics has been treated as a special theological discipline, recent studies have endeavored to enlarge the scope of hermeneutics. These studies wish to see hermeneutics in a wider perspective as a function of the human understanding (German: *Verstehen*, the grasping of meaning in depth in contrast to *Erkärung* which is merely technical explanation). Understanding is the capacity which people have to give and receive meaning. When a person speaks or writes he gives meaning; when he listens or reads he receives meaning. Hermeneutics is then deeply imbedded in the larger structure of communication. Stemming from Schleiermacher, Dilthey, and Heidegger there has arisen a new movement in hermeneutics which is so comprehensive that it is a philosophy and a theology (Fuchs, Ebeling, Gadamer). Within this larger comprehension of hermeneutics is the more technical kind of hermeneutics known as sacred or Biblical hermeneutics. In this article our concern is with the latter.

When a person is familiar with the materials he reads or hears the process of understanding occurs without effort. Interpretation is present but it functions so spontaneously that it is not evident. When a person is confronted with strange materials his process of understanding becomes self-conscious. An effort is made to find rules that will guide the interpreter through such materials. These rules are necessary because interpretation is as much art as it is science, and therefore there must be protection against arbitrary interpretation made in the name of art. Arbitrary interpretation may be a wrenching of the truth of the text or it may be the overapplication of a legitimate procedure (as in typological interpretation). The conscious setting up of rules is hermeneutics (from the god Hermes, messenger of the gods, hence *hermēneuein,* to interpret; *hermēneia,* interpretation, commentary; and *hē hermēneutikē technē,* the skill or art of interpretation).

General hermeneutics is that set of rules employed in all materials which stand in need of interpretation. It is used, with proper adaption to the subject matter, in art, history, literature, archeology and translation. Something stands in need of interpretation when something hinders its spontaneous understanding. To put it another way a gap exists between the interpreter and the materials to be interpreted and rules must be set up to bridge this gap. In that the interpreter is separated from his materials in time there is a historical gap; in that his culture is different from that of his text there is a cultural gap; in that the text is usually in a different language there is the linguistic gap; in that the document originates in another country there is the geological gap and the biological gap (the flora and fauna). In that usually a totally different attitude towards life and the universe exists in the text it can be said that there is a philosophical gap (German: *Weltanschauung,* the metaphysical manner in which the universe is put together; *Weltbild,* the physical [scientific or pseudo-scientific] manner in which the universe is put together).

Biblical hermeneutics is the study of those principles which pertain to the interpretation of Holy Scripture. In that all of the usual gaps exist between the interpreter and the text of Scripture rules for interpretation are mandatory. In that the Holy Scripture has some problems peculiar to itself (e.g., the relationship of the Old to the New Testament), other principles are necessary for the complete system of Biblical hermeneutics.

Biblical hermeneutics is capable of further division. Some works on hermeneutics present the hermeneutics of the Old Testament, then of the New Testament. Others speak of general hermeneutics as the ascertaining of those principles which apply to the entire Bible, and special hermeneutics as those principles which apply to special literary segments of the Bible (e.g., prophecy, parables).

Hermeneutics is both an art and a science. It is a science in that it can reduce interpretation within limits to a set of rules; it is an art in that not infrequently elements in the text escape easy treatment by rules. Some writers have argued that the giving and taking of meaning in understanding

(*Verstehen*) is more art than science. But at least it is not all art and what is not art can be treated by rule.

It has been customary to specify hermeneutics as the theory of interpretation and exegesis as the application of the theory to the text. Hermeneutics studies the theory of interpretation and refers to exegesis only to illustrate its points. Exegesis deals concretely with the text and refers to hermeneutics only to argue a point. But recent studies in hermeneutics indicate that hermeneutical principles are distilled from the activity of exegesis itself. Therefore any division between exegesis and hermeneutics is somewhat artificial. Scholars did not develop a theory of hermeneutics from abstract considerations, but the practical issues of exegesis (as well as controversy in interpretation) drove them to the formulation of hermeneutical theory.

Hermeneutics, exegesis, and preaching form one continuum. The minister who stands in the tradition of the Reformation that the minister is the minister of the Word of God (*ministerium verbi divine*) believes that the center of gravity in his ministry is the Word of God. This means that the greatest responsibility of a ministry is the ministry of the Word of God to the congregation. Preaching must be centered in the interpretation and application of Holy Scripture. The message from the pulpit will be Biblical, exegetical, and expository. Holy Scripture is the source and norm of preaching; exegesis is the scientific ascertaining of the meaning of the text; and exposition is its relevant proclamation to the congregation. The concept which binds these three together is the concept of the Word of God. The Scripture is the Word of God written; exegesis is the Word of God understood; and preaching is the Word of God made relevant to time and place. This high view of preaching as an important form of the Word of God is in keeping with the high view of preaching maintained at the time of the Reformation by both Luther and Calvin.

Exegesis and exposition bear a special relationship to each other. Exposition grows out of exegesis. In exegesis the preacher concentrates on the meaning of the text *historically* understood. He is not immediately concerned with the relevance for the present generation. In so bracketing off present concern he is free from all those forces that would distort his search for the meaning of the text whether these forces be social, ecclesiastical, or political. Illustrative of this point were the researches of Luther into the original meaning of the Psalms, Galatians, Romans and Hebrews. In exposition the minister is concerned with the application and relevance of the text for the contemporary generation — again illustrated by Luther who made the text relevant to his day and so started the Reformation. Exegesis without application is academic; exposition that is not grounded in exegesis is either superficial or misleading or even both.

There must be no separation of exegesis and application. The twentieth century has witnessed too many instances in which exegesis was carried on without fulfilling itself in application. Christians could have had any number of cell Bible studies and never passed judgment on the Hitler regime. Christians all over the world may enjoy their in-group Bible study and ignore the grave political, social, and racial injustices and evils that surround them. Application is not a second and dispensable activity after exegesis, but in the normal situation exegesis leads inevitably to application.

If the Word of God is the center of the ministry then the minister must treat his text exegetically before he treats it homiletically. If he is to be a responsible exegete he must have a responsible working theory of Biblical hermeneutics. Otherwise his exegesis will be willy-nilly and uneven. This will reflect itself in the quality of one's preaching. Therefore if the minister is to be a faithful steward of the Word of God he must have a mature working theory of Biblical hermeneutics as the basis of his homiletics.

2. GENERAL BIBLICAL HERMENEUTICS

In that Holy Scripture is to a large measure similar to other literature the science of general hermeneutics is applicable to Biblical hermeneutics. The point of beginning in Biblical hermeneutics is to explore how the principles of general hermeneutics apply to it.

Prior to the minister's actual working with the text itself he has already made certain fundamental decisions. He has, for example, a certain conviction about the theological nature of Holy Scripture. To him the Scripture is the Word of God written which has been the universal faith of the church regardless of particular theories of inspiration, and regardless of debates whether the Bible *is* or *contains* the Word of God. Holy Scripture had its origin in the divine speaking and acting; it was transmitted to the prophets and apostles who were special agents of divine revelation; and it was cast into writing by the process of divine inspiration. This is not a dry, rational faith in a static body of literature. The evangelical preacher believes in the animating power of the Word of God, and in the quickening power of the Holy Spirit. He knows that in every generation the Word of God is to be brought to a new hearing by more vigorous exegesis and fruitful application. From the same Word of God came Augustine's great critique of pagan culture; Thomas' great attempt at synthesis of reason and revelation in the Middle Ages; and Luther's great reformulation of the Christian gospel.

This Word of God the evangelical minister accepts in the canon of Holy Scripture. The canon is the list of books which the church has deemed part of the organism of revelation and therefore the divine authority within the church. The Protestant minister works with the canon that came out of the Reformation (but not in blind unawareness of the critical problems of canon formation). The concept of the Word of God determines the concept of a canon; the historical formulation of the canon was a human decision in which it is believed that the Holy Spirit was operative.

The evangelical minister works with an accepted critical edition of the Hebrew Old Testament and the Greek New Testament. As a general rule he trusts the scholarship that has striven to give the church the purest text possible. If a preacher is not competent in the original languages he must use English translations that are based upon a critical text of the original languages as the American Standard Version and the Revised Standard Version. If the minister prefers for personal reasons to preach from the King James Version he must at least acquaint himself with the variant readings attested in the other English versions of the Holy Scripture.

Textual criticism is to be followed by a study of Biblical introduction as it relates to the text to be interpreted. The routine matters of Biblical introduction are concerned with authorship, dates, where the book was written, who were its recipients, and the conditions that prompted the writing of the book. In that each book of the Bible has its own set of critical problems the interpreter will inform himself of these. Only as the book is set in its wider historical and literary perspectives can justice be done to it in its interpretation.

At this point it is now possible to discuss those principles of general hermeneutics which carry over into Biblical hermeneutics.

a. *Literary Genre.* In the interpretation of a literary text the first matter to be concretely settled is its *literary genre.* It is the literary genre of the text which determines the frame of reference in which the words are used, and therefore the frame of reference is logically prior to the words. Some Scripture is poetry, some proverbs, some history, some sermonic, some parables, etc. The determination of the literary genre of the text determines the interpreter's mood and stance.

b. *Word Study.* Once the literary genre of a passage has been settled the piecemeal work of exegesis begins. It usually begins with a study of words because the word is the ultimate unit of meaning. There are various ways words can be studied. Words can be studied *etymologically.* The knowledge of the components of a word and its formation may be instrumental in unlocking its meaning. Words can be studied *comparatively.* Words usually occur many places in Scripture and tracing a word through a concordance is basic home work for good exegesis. There are Hebrew and Greek concordances and critical concordances as Strong and Young that aid the person who does not know the original languages. Bible dictionaries and theological word books are also sources of information about major Biblical words. There is some merit in studying synonyms for it reveals what words the writers of Scripture considered blood relatives. Words may be studied *historically* (*usus loquendi*). We have the classic example of this kind of research in Kittel's famous *Theological Dictionary of the New Testament* (in process of translation from the German). A word is studied in its classical Greek usage;

then in the Hebrew Bible; then in the Septuagint; then in the inter-Biblical period with special regard to the Aramaic; then comprehensively in the Greek New Testament; and in some instances in the early Patristic literature. The historical study of words always includes research in cognate languages and in the great translations of the Old and New Testaments of antiquity.

It would be unrealistic to expect a parish minister to do extensive research in Biblical words. But there are things he can do to compensate for this. He can develop a sensitivity to words as such in the English language and make extensive use of an unabridged dictionary. He can use the latest lexicons which classify most of the uses of the Hebrew and Greek words. Bauer spent a life time to give us an accurate classification of the words of the Greek New Testament (in Arndt and Gingrich's translation, *A Greek English Lexicon of the New Testament*).

c. *Grammatical Exegesis.* The study of words is helpful but limited. It is grammatical exegesis which presses on to the interpretation of the sentence in all its parts, and the paragraph composed of sentences. Its corollary is the priority of the literal (or normal) sense of Scripture (in opposition to the medieval scheme of the fourfold meaning of the sense of Scripture). It is neither possible nor necessary to discuss the grammar of the Biblical languages at this point.

Grammatical exegesis is sometimes called literal exegesis. By the literal meaning of words and phrases is meant their normal, natural, customary sense *in situ* in their language. Allegorical exegesis has been the bedevilment of exegesis. It was the Christocentric character of allegorical exegesis in the Patristic period which saved it from being pure trash. The Reformers saw correctly that only in literal exegesis could the church be purged from centuries of accretions in the interpretation of Scripture. Literal exegesis is the check upon all irresponsible exegesis whether it be found in the history of the church or in some contemporary cult.

Grammatical exegesis pays very strict attention to the context of a passage. It has been well said that the context of every text is the canon. There is also the context of the Old or New Testament, the context of the book, the context of the chapter, and the context of the paragraph. Paul uses the word law (*nomos*) so flexibly that its particular meaning can be settled only by appeal to the context.

The next stage in grammatical exegesis is to turn to the cultural elements in the text such as references to persons, events, social practices, matters of geography (cities, towns, rivers, mountains, etc.), and flora and fauna. This is not only a matter of learning the particular items mentioned in the text but it involves the attempt to create the political and sociological world of the past. Why were the Galatians easy victims for the Judaizers? Why did the church at Corinth become the church of ecstatic gifts? What kind of community received the epistle to the Hebrews? When were certain Psalms apt to be used in liturgy? These are the sort of comprehensive questions the interpreter must ask to bring the text to its fullest hearing.

Again it must be conceded that it is impossible for the parish minister to search out all of these matters. The best recourse for the minister is to turn to a good commentary, for a good commentary will be concerned with all the things we have mentioned here. It will give him an introduction to the book. It will discuss important textual variations. It will have excellent studies of the more important words and items of grammar. It will supply the user with good historical and cultural materials. As a rule of thumb it may be said that good hermeneutics is the use of good commentaries, and bad hermeneutics is their neglect.

The commentator on Scripture has a wide range of commentaries to draw upon. Each serves a distinct purpose from the very technical commentary with its wealth of lexical and grammatical materials to the more homiletical and devotional with their general assessments of the theological, spiritual, and practical implications of the text. Again as a most general rule it can be said that newer commentaries are better than old ones, and critical and grammatical ones will be more rewarding over the years than popular and devotional ones.

3. HERMENEUTICAL PRINCIPLES SPECIAL TO SCRIPTURE

In many ways Holy Scripture is one piece with other literature. It is written in common languages; it uses many typical forms of literary composition; it refers to thousands of matters of common experience; and much of its history is buried amidst other histories. In all these matters in which the Bible overlaps other literature it is to be interpreted as other literature. But the Holy Scripture has certain unique features which require special principles if full justice is to be done to the interpretation of Scripture.

a. *The Spiritual Factor*. It was Calvin who noted that the Word of God is spiritual and therefore could only be spiritually perceived. It was for this reason that he broke with a rationalistic apologetic that presumed that it could prove Christianity to be true by an appeal to human reason as such. There are two sides to the spirituality of the Word of God. God moves upon man by the Holy Spirit who illuminates the mind and witnesses to the veracity of the divine verities. But the man upon whom the Spirit moves must be a partaker of the Spirit in regeneration. The Scriptures are most likely to be understood when a regenerate man trusts the Holy Spirit to illuminate his mind as he interprets Scripture. Relying on the Spirit is no substitute for learning. It must be conceded that an ignorant Christian is no match for a learned unbeliever. Reliance upon the Spirit must always be in conjunction with the best possible procedures in exegesis.

Those who wish a strictly controlled scientific exegesis, or who believe that in view of the "historicity" of the text the text is understandable exhaustively by general hermeneutics, look upon spiritual considerations as illicit intrusion of the subjective into an area where it does not belong. They do not see how recourse to the Holy Spirit has operational value. If objective criteria are not forthcoming, the role of the Spirit in exegesis is rejected as subjectivism or pietism. But the issue is not so easily settled. The subjective disposition of a scholar weighs heavily upon him in his exegesis. Communists have no sympathy with existentialism, and interpret it as the dying gasp of a decadent capitalism. Marx's complete preoccupation with economics caused him to recast the philosophy of Hegel into a fantastic perversion of Hegel. Logical positivists of the old school showed only disdain for metaphysics, poetry, and religion. The scholar does not exist who is completely free from presuppositions, and completely delivered from any emotionally or culturally rooted disposition that would materially influence his interpretations.

If subjective disposition plays such a decisive role in all interpretation (in spite of the best intentions to be "scientific" or "objective"), then the subjective disposition in Biblical exegesis is of immense importance. That the Holy Spirit might significantly effect the subjective disposition of the exegete and thereby his exegesis, cannot be ruled out of court even though it is not possible to give criteria for the Spirit's action. The intangibility of the work of the Spirit might be far more real than all the scientific procedures applied to the text. Because it is believed that the great fathers of the church were

Spirit-gifted men some theologians trust more to patristic exegesis than they do to modern scientific exegesis. Others think that Luther and Calvin were such men of the Spirit that they are better guides to the real substance of the New Testament then men of our day with all their aids to exegesis.

b. *The Unity of Scripture.* The unity of Scripture and the harmony of Scripture is Jesus Christ and the redemption and revelation which centers in him. Hermeneutics has always been caught between Origen and Marcion. In Marcion we have an unChristian reduction of the Old Testament, and in Origen a Christian inflation of the Old Testament. The balance between the Old and New Testaments was one of the most difficult hermeneutical issues of the Reformation. The battle continues today in that Bultmann stands for a Marcion interpretation of the Old Testament, while Barth retains a Christological exegesis of the Old Testament.

Although the church may not be able to neatly solve the particular problems of Old Testament exegesis it nevertheless believes that the Old Testament is essentially a Christian book. The one theme of both Testaments is Jesus Christ and his redemption. It is admitted that the presence of Christ in the Old Testament is not fully clear, and therefore the Christological exegesis of the Old Testament will never be free from difficulty. In spite of the fantasies of allegorical exegesis its heart was in the right place in insisting on the Christian content of the Old Testament.

In that the New Testament is the realization of the Old a special hermeneutical principle is necessary. For the Christian church the center of gravity of the Scriptures is the New Testament. In the New Testament is recorded the incarnation, the life of the incarnate Son, the saving events of the cross and the resurrection, and the interpretation of the person and work of Christ in the epistles. The granting of the priority of the New Testament over the Old Testament is not meant to be an enervating relativization of the Old Testament. The Old Testament stands in a right of its own and many of its great passages are without parallel in the New Testament (e.g., Psalm 23). That which the principle intends to grant is the priority of the New Testament in the theological understanding of salvation and the Christian life.

c. *Progressive Revelation.* The concept of progressive revelation is based upon the conviction that revelation and redemption move along a historical line and that this historical line has a certain character to it. The most obvious division of the line is its division into the Old Testament period and the New Testament period. Even in the New Testament period there is division between the events prior to Pentecost and those after Pentecost. There is a progression in Scripture and unless this principle of progression is recognized there can be no clear exegesis of Scripture.

Progressive revelation means that God takes man where he finds him and with whatever notions he has of God and ethical principles and seeks to lead him higher and higher. If revelation is to make contact with empirical man it must meet him where he is. The primeval concepts of man about God and morality is a witness of God reaching down to empirical man where he is. Progressive revelation also means that as the time line unravels, the purposes of God become clearer and fuller. It involves the enlargement of the idea of God, the purification of ethical ideals, the spiritualizing of worship, and progress in divine redemption. It is because of progressive revelation that the church has found its fulness of revelation, its supreme doctrine of God, its climax of revelation, and its final ethical imperatives in the New Testament and not the Old.

Programmatically this means two things to the interpreter. If there is any tension between the older revelation and the newer, the older must give way to the newer. Although there are some remarkable ethical materials in the Old Testament, Christian theology must consciously build its final ethical formulations from the New Testament. Furthermore, it means that there is no uniformity of importance in the Scriptures. It is true that in so-called scholastic orthodoxy, Scriptures were cited as proofs without regard to their location in Scripture (hence a passing reference in the Psalms was given as much weight as a verse in Romans). But this kind of exegesis is no longer defensible and has all but disappeared in contemporary theology. The locus of a text in the corpus of revelation determines the mode of its exegesis and the theological weight that can be assessed to it.

d. *The Self-interpretation of Scripture.* At the time of the Reformation the Roman Catholic Church insisted that it was gifted with the grace of interpretation and therefore it knew instinctively the intention of Scripture. The Reformers rejected this claim and set in its place the rule that Scripture is its own interpreter (*Scriptura sacra sui ipsius interpres*). That which raised this issue was the problem created by the darker or more difficult passages of Scripture. Luther taught the objective clarity of Scripture to be Jesus Christ, and the subjective clarity to be the Holy Spirit. But this did not mean all the Bible was clear. The Catholics appealed to their gift of interpretation to direct its way through the darker part of Scripture. The Reformers appealed to "Scripture interprets Scripture." Obviously the word "Scripture" is used in two senses in this catch phrase. What it means is that the *whole* of Scripture interprets the *part* of Scripture and thus no part of Scripture can be so interpreted as to deform the teaching of the whole of Scripture. Thus incidental references in Scripture cannot be made pillars of truth. One of the most familiar traits of a sect is that it carries on this very sort of exegesis.

"Scripture interprets Scripture" has also been called the hermeneutical circle. The *whole* of Scripture can be learned only by interpreting it *part* by *part*. No man's attention span is so great that he can ingest the whole Scripture at once. Yet no part can stand in isolation from the whole. So the interpreter must go the circle from part to whole and from whole to part.

Another version of the hermeneutical circle is to be found in the Bultmann circle. The Scripture is understood only as the exegete asks leading questions of the text; but in working with the text the exegete is himself questioned by the text. But this questioning by the text gives him a deeper existential insight so now he knows how to better question the text. Hence he moves in the circle of questioning and in turn being questioned and in turn questioning the text.

e. *The Supernatural in Scripture.* The evangelical expositor accepts the report of the supernatural in the text. Since the time of the founding of modern science and modern philosophy, educated secular man has been opposed to Christian supernaturalism. To him the only factors in the universe are the immanent laws of nature. Since the time of the German enlightenment many theologians have taken the same stance with reference to theology and the Scriptures. The result of this attitude upon the interpretation of Scripture is that all reports of the supernatural in Scripture are written off as some kind of misunderstanding. Such anti-supernatural scholars point out that in precritical cultures the supernatural is everywhere. Therefore it ought not to surprise us if we find the supernatural reported in the Scriptures for they were written in precritical times. Exegesis accordingly treats the report of the supernatural in Scriptures as it would in any document of Greek or Roman antiquity which reported a supernatural event.

The evangelical Christian believes that there is a radical difference between the report of the supernatural in Scripture and in other literature. There is a sober rationale for the supernatural in Scripture based upon the Biblical structure of revelation and redemption which is completely lacking in precritical cultures. The Christian considers the present order to be out of joint and unnatural due to sin. Part of God's revelatory and redemptive work in a humanity and cosmos darkened by sin is the employment of the supernatural. Therefore when the evangelical expositor is confronted with the supernatural in the text he does not rule it out *ex hypothesi,* but accepts it as an important element of the Biblical revelation.

f. *Theological Exegesis.* The evangelical expositor is interested in the fullest reaches of Biblical interpretation and this leads to the necessary theological exegesis of the text. This is not a *double* treatment of the text as if first the text is given a grammatical interpretation and then a "spiritual" (*pneumatische*) interpretation. Theological exegesis can be nothing else but the extension of the line of grammatical exegesis. It is true that there has been in the history of the church this doubling of exegesis. It was true in Patristic times when the allegorical interpretation of the text was superimposed on the grammatical meaning of the text. It is true in contemporary times in Paul Tillich who forces an existential calculus on the text which is foreign to its grammatical sense.

Theological exegesis extends grammatical exegesis in that theological exegesis is interested in the largest implications of the text. Propositions imply other propositions. In formal systems (logic, mathematics, geometry), the process of drawing propositions from other propositions is strictly controlled. In material systems (science, history, psychology, etc.), the implications of a proposition are not always obvious and the verification of a proposition may be very difficult. The Bible as a literary and historical document does not belong to the formal system but to the material. Therefore deducing propositions from Scripture faces all of the problems typical of deducing propositions in a material system.

Although no hard line may be drawn between grammatical exegesis and theological exegesis it may be programmatically said that theological exegesis takes up where grammatical exegesis leaves off and seeks to find the fuller implications of the text. For this reason it is forced to used concepts (logical constructs) that would not be used in grammatical exegesis (e.g., original sin, total depravity, communion of natures, etc.), and this accounts for the rather startling difference of vocabulary beween grammatical exegesis and systematic theology. The great theologian differs from the ordinary theologian in the former's ability to draw out these larger implications of the text. It was in men like Augustine, Luther, Calvin, and Barth that the genius of theological exegesis came into its own.

In that theological exegesis deals with this creative extension of the meaning of the text it is not as strictly controllable as grammatical exegesis. Theological exegesis is more art than technique, and insight is more important to it than the linguistic details of grammatical exegesis. The proof of the pudding is in the eating and the ultimate justification of theological exegesis must be its ability to make the text meaningful in its greatest depth.

The second character of theological exegesis is that the canon of Scripture is the context of every passage of Scripture. This is the theological version of "Scripture interprets Scripture." The exegete brings all the other materials that are similar to the text to bear upon the text. Again this procedure is as much art and insight as it is exegesis. Therefore it is not easy to control.

In recent times Barth has endeavored to pioneer theological exegesis in a fresh way. To him the entire Bible is the context for each passage and therefore he has no hesitancy in bringing items from the history of Israel and the New Testament into his interpretation of Genesis 1. Or in some event of the Old Testament or in some person of the Old Testament he sees a gold mine of theological materials because he brings other parts of Scripture to this text and inflates it so to speak. Although Barth has been accused of allegorical exegesis and of spiritualizing the text he nevertheless at least gives us one version of theological exegesis. His particular exegesis may be seriously questioned, but his notion of exegesis as demanding that the entire text of the Bible be brought to bear on particular texts is sound.

BIBLIOGRAPHY

Ebeling, Gerhard, "Hermeneutik," *Religion in Geschichte und Gegenwart,* (third edition), III, 242-262.

Frör, Kurt, *Biblische Hermenutik.* Munich: Chr. Kaiser, 1961.

Mickelsen, A. Berkeley, *Interpreting the Bible.* Grand Rapids: Wm. B. Eerdmans, 1963.

Ramm, Bernard, *Protestant Biblical Interpretation* (revised edition). Boston: W. A. Wilde, 1956.

Smart, James, *The Interpretation of Scripture.* Philadelphia: Westminster Press, 1961.

Terry, Milton, *Biblical Hermeneutics.* New edition; New York: Eaton and Mains, 1883.

Weber, Otto, *Grundlagen der Dogmatik.* First edition; Neukirchen: Verlag der Buchhandlung des Erziehungsvereins, 1955. Vol. I, pp. 341-384.

2

Interpretation of Parables

A parable is an extended metaphor or simile which compares a religious truth with a common experience or circumstance in life. As a didactic device its roots are to be traced to the Old Testament where it is found mainly in Proverbs. The Greek word *parabolic* is found nearly fifty times in the Gospels in connection with the teaching ministry of Jesus. Therefore, the parable was obviously a favorite and central teaching instrument of Jesus. In this respect he stood with the rabbis who also made extensive use of the parable. However, two features distinguish Jesus' parabolic teaching from that of the rabbis: (1) Jesus' parables were marked by freshness, simplicity and creativity, whereas those of the rabbis tended towards the ponderous and pedantic; and (2) Jesus' parables related to the coming kingdom, while the parables of the rabbis focused upon the Torah and its manifold implications.

1. RELATIONSHIP TO ALLEGORY

Because parable and allegory share many common attributes, from earliest times confusion has existed within these two literary genres with the unhappy result that parabolic interpretation has been allegorized, and the distinctive thrust of the parabolic form has been attenuated and often eclipsed. Briefly stated, a parable exists to establish one point, so that individual details serve this one purpose and have no great significance in themselves. On the other hand, an allegory may establish several points by virtue of the meaningfulness of the several details which comprise the allegory. Perhaps the outstanding example of allegory in the New Testament is found in Paul's discussion of Hagar and Sarah in Galatians 4:21-31. However, it should be noted that this custom is rare and furthermore, Paul specifically identified his handling of the theme as an allegory (vs. 24). The allegorization of the parables of Jesus commenced perhaps even within New Testament times, but its greatest development took place under Origen who, following the hermeneutical scheme of Philo, adopted allegorization as the most fruitful method of Biblical interpretation. His baneful influence affected not only the church fathers for centuries, but continues up to the present, especially in the interpretation of the parables of Jesus.

The dominating hold of allegory upon parabolic interpretation was broken by the German theologian A. Jülicher (*Die Gleichnisreden Jesu*, 1888). He rightly perceived the difference between allegory and parable, affirming that the latter teaches one central point, all elements of a parable being secondary and subordinate to that one point. His thesis that the parables are distinct from allegory, and are to be interpreted differently, is a major contribution to this area of investigation and is of lasting value. The later labors of C. H. Dodd (*The Parables of the Kingdom*, 1936) and J. Jeremias (*The Parables of Jesus*, 1954), while they modify some of the puristic overclassifications of Juulicher, rest upon and proceed from his work. Since Juulicher's time it has come to be recognized that he differentiated too sharply between allegory, metaphor, simile, and parable. As literary and oral didactic genres which evolved out of dynamic human situations, these forms inevitably blend at some points. It should be remembered that the Old Testament prophets, the rabbis, and Jesus were not concerned with scholastic niceties of classification and were not therefore obliged to follow rules of distinction. On the other hand, the expounder today has no right to ignore the proper characteristics of a parable and proceed to allegorize upon it. With good reason the allegorical scheme has been called the "wax nose" method of interpretation because of the uncontrollable nature of allegory which gives free reign to every vagrant imagination about the sense of the text. Allegorizing of parables has for centuries been a source of mischief to correct historical interpretation of the parables of Jesus.

2. TYPES OF PARABLES

Jesus exercised considerable freedom within the general parabolic style so that it is difficult to type his sayings with systematic precision. In general, three types may be discerned: (1) short, pithy similes which vividly characterize someone or something, e.g., salt of the earth, light of the world, blind leaders of the blind, lamp on a stand; (2) a saying which explains a normal event in life, e.g., the servant is not greater than his master, you cannot serve God and mammon, the kingdom of heaven is like a net; (3) the lengthier narrative parable which has no formula of comparison and which is a fully worked out story in itself, e.g., the good samaritan (Luke 10:30-37), the prodigal son (Luke 15:11-32), the wedding feast (Matt. 22:1-14), the sower (Mark 4:3-8), the great supper (Luke 14:16-24), the rich man and Lazarus (Luke 16:19-31), the pharisee and the publican (Luke 18:9-14). It should be borne in mind that not only do the parables defy strict classification, but also at times, especially in John, it is difficult to decide whether a given saying is a parable or an allegory, as in the example of the vine and the branches (John 15:1f.). As a rule, a parable exhibits a formal, stylized introduction, expecially in the cases of the sayings about a normal event of everyday life, and the narrative parable. In the one, the introductory formula is "The kingdom of heaven is like . . .," and in the second, "A certain man. . . ." Such formulae are useful for identification of a parable and the consequent method of interpretation applied to it. One of the chief examples of difficulty of classification is the parable of the sower (Mark 4:3-8). It is generally agreed that the central point is that the proclamation of the gospel elicits a wide variety of responses from the hearers. The controversy exists, however, over verses 10-

23 which are alleged in the text to be Jesus' own interpretation of the parable. Many critics assert that this is an example of Mark's editorializing tendency to explain Jesus' words. Some scholars go so far as to state that Mark failed to understand the nature of a parable, and hopelessly allegorized the original parable of Jesus. Over against this view it may be urged that Jesus was not bound by modern literary distinctions, and could in fact have allegorized his own parable, much as appears to have been done in the story about the vine and the branches. This possibility, however, is not free of difficulty for the reason of its rarity within the synoptic gospels.

3. VARIED USE OF PARABLES

An analysis of the way Jesus' parables are reported and couched in the Gospels, especially the synoptics, reveals that each evangelist handled an original saying of Jesus with some latitude and variety, depending upon the general purpose of the context. That they did not observe rigid rules of reportorial precision, either in respect to the words of Jesus or to the context in which they were originally uttered, will prove disagreeable to some because it leads to a diminution of confidence in the historical reliability of the gospels themselves. However this may be, it is undeniable that such shaping and alteration of Jesus' words did in fact take place. A clear example of this editorializing interest is seen in a comparative study of the parables of the great supper (Luke 14:16-24) and the wedding feast

(Matt. 22:1-14). Originally this was one parable spoken by Jesus which Matthew adapted to a court setting which mirrors by implication some of the Jewish-Christian controversy at the time of the writing of this gospel, whereas Luke's interest is almost purely eschatological, anticipatory of the messianic banquet. Various details are altered so that the servants in Matthew's narrative are the prophets but in Luke's account the servant is Jesus. The central point in both accounts is the same: many are invited to the table of God, but not all will come. It might be argued that both gospels preserve two independent sayings. This is formally possible. But it is clear that adaptation and variation of reporting did take place among the several evangelists. The baptism, temptation, sermon on the mount, transfiguration, crucifixion, and resurrection narratives all vary in individual details. Of critical importance is not whether the evangelists preserved accuracy in specific detail, but substantial fact. Two further examples will illustrate this tendency by the evangelists Matthew 5:25-26 and Luke 12:58-59 contain the parable of the man who must appear before a judge. Luke's interest is again eschatological, anticipating the day of judgment before God. On the other hand, Matthew's interest is directed to the requirements of human legal procedures; it is prudential morality which is uppermost in Matthew's mind as he adapted Jesus' original saying to this new purpose. Indeed, Matthew's mode of handling this parable is suggestive of the inclination in early times to make a parable assume a hortatory purpose. Matthew 13 is well-known for its collection of parables on the kingdom. There is no claim in Matthew's Gospel, nor is there any sound reason to infer, that these parables were recorded verbatim, or in the order that Jesus uttered them. Moreover, there is no reason to assume that Jesus spoke all these parables in one sermon; the movement of thought in Matthew's Gospel strongly suggests that the collection as it stands in the text bears strong evidence of Matthew's own redactional work and that it reflects his own interest to a remarkable degree. This point is supported by the fact that there is no parallel collection of kingdom parables in any of the other gospels.

This powerful evidence of adaptation in Jesus' original parabolic teaching is highly instructive for preaching on the parables today. It is perfectly clear that the gospel writers held Jesus' words to be inspired and therefore authoritative and objects of deepest reverence, but this did not mean that his words could not be reshaped to new circumstances and demands. This raises a highly significant point: to be meaningful a parable must always be interpreted in the light of new historical contexts in which the Word of God is expounded. This is not to give license to unbridled and incautious vulgarizing of Jesus' words. Rather, it means that the preacher today, as in every generation, must examine the parable as it stands in the text, ascertain as closely as possible the original setting of the parable and then make a thoughtful, penetrating application of that parable to the spiritual context of his hearers. Otherwise, preaching on the parables is simply debased either to fascinating vignettes of life in ancient Palestine, or to moralisms, neither of which is authentic proclamation of the Word of God. To make an impact upon the modern hearer, the parables of Jesus must respond to a contemporary demand and situation.

4. ESCHATOLOGICAL NATURE OF THE PARABLES

If the burden of the parables of Jesus can be summed up in one word, it would be "eschatology." It used to be the fashion to read his words as teaching the progressive improvement of the human condition by human means. Nothing could be further from the truth of Jesus' intention, for by the parables he taught the imminent inbreaking of God's sovereign and redeeming purpose in the world. Nor did Jesus relate his parables with any intellectualistic goals, as though he were speaking some kind of abstract, timeless verity in an enigmatic manner. His interest was not in mental games and riddles, but with the kingdom of God which was dawning with a new day of redemption in his own person and ministry.

Three features of this eschatological kingdom assert themselves repeatedly in the parabolic ministry of Jesus. First, the coming of the kingdom is near. Mark 1:14 f. records Jesus' opening words in his public ministry as a call to repentance because of the nearness of the kingdom, and this theme reasserts inself in many of his parables. Of course, the presence of Jesus was itself the guarantee of the nearness of the kingdom, for he was the agent by whom the kingdom was made present and effective in the world. Therefore, the parables, like the miracles, are a sign of Jesus' deity and unique relationship to the Father. The hidden and coming glory of the kingdom of God are contained in, and progressively revealed by, Jesus Christ, the eternal Word. Secondly, the imminence of the kingdom implies a separation within the human family, some to sorrow and judgment, and some to joy and final redemption. The note of joy and delight at the revelation of God's saving intention is uppermost in Jesus' mind, for its arrival signals relief for the oppressed and restoration for the downtrodden, an emphasis found particularly in Luke. Thirdly, the eschatological character of the kingdom means that it commences with small, insignificant and inauspicious beginnings, but its end is all-encompassing, powerful and transcendent. This could be said to parallel the life of Christ and the life of the church. The promise contained in this eschatological kingdom is the final victory of God's kingdom over every opponent, tyranny, and hostility directed against God's will and sway over the created order. God's will shall be done on earth as it is in heaven.

5. THE PURPOSE OF THE PARABLES

Cognate with the nature of parable is its function. Again, Jesus was not primarily concerned with intellectual stimulation as such, but with the moral response of his audience upon hearing the parable. It was not perception of some deep, esoteric truth by his hearers, but a decisive response of repentance, faith, hope, and love that motivated Jesus' use of parables. Therefore, his parables may be likened to arrows which were aimed at man's heart, the core of his being, the place of his will and affections. Just as the entire weight and momentum of an arrow make their impact felt at one decisive point, so Jesus' parables rested their full weight upon a relentless, searching claim upon man's heart. Apocalyptic speculations, facile moralisms, and intellectualistic diversions constituted no part of Jesus' purpose in parabolic teaching. Instead, he sought to confront his hearers with the ineluctable, implacable and gracious claim of God upon the soul of man.

As in the case of miracles, so also parables elicited a variety of responses, for both miracle and parable were greeted with reactions ranging all the way from scorn and derision to contrition and faith. Mark 4:11 and simliar passages appear to teach that God positively hardened the hearts of some hearers and warmed the hearts of others so they could respond with faith. A better understanding of such passages takes Jesus' words as stating a gnomic fact: faith comes to him whose spirit is ready and open, and it is withheld from the proud and scornful. This is no attempt to analyze the final mystery of the tides and impulses of human decision. It may only be observed that parables in fact accomplish two ends: revelation

and concealment, understanding and nonun-
derstanding.

6. SUGGESTIONS FOR A PRACTICAL
METHOD OF PREACHING ON THE
PARABLES

a. Examine the parable closely to recon-
struct the real situation in which and to
which Jesus spoke his parable. What questions were put to him? What were his answers? Who asked the questions? Why did
the questioners put the query to Jesus? The
answer to such questions will show that
Jesus avoided vague, banal generalities, and
aimed his parable at specific human needs
and challenges.

b. Analyze the parable for the unusual
element in the story. Local color will lead
the hearer to the spiritual intention of Jesus.

c. The point of the parable is often found
in the last sentence of the story. Many times
the homely, pungent thrust of a parable is
missed in a search for some elusive and
"deeper" meaning. The expositor should be
willing to see the obvious.

d. A parable has one point. As an arrow
has one point and one area of impact, so
has a parable. A failure to focus all the
force of the parable upon its one point will
result in dissipation of its power. Be sure to
isolate and expound the unique gift of each
parable.

e. Interpretation and application of the
ancient parable is a never-ending task, but
great are its rewards. The expounder of the

parable must not only know the parable, its circumstances and its theological weight, but he must also be sensitized to his own time, his generation, his world, and his congregation which has its ever-changing fears, demands, burdens, and aspirations.

BIBLIOGRAPHY

Dodd, C. H., *The Parables of the Kingdom,* 1936.
Frör, K., *Biblische Hermeneutik.*
Jeremias, J., *The Parables of the Kingdom,* 1954.
Jülicher, A., *Die Gleichnisreden Jesu,* 1888.

3

Old Testament Quotations in the New Testament

The first factor that is to be considered is the sheer mass of New Testament quotations of or allusions to the Old Testament. Roughly one-tenth of the New Testament is really Old Testament material. This proportion holds also in the recorded words of Jesus. One may gather a general impression in this area by perusing an edition of the New Testament like the Nestle *Greek Testament*, where Old Testament quotations and reminiscences are printed in boldface type. Such a perusal would make it apparent that the heaviest concentration of Old Testament materials is to be found in Revelation, Romans, and Hebrews.

A conservative count discloses some 295 separate explicit references to the Old Testament. These occupy some 352 verses of the New Testament. 278 different verses of the Old Testament are cited (some more than once, hence the difference in numbering), 94 from the "Torah" or Pentateuch, 99 from the "Prophets," and 85 from the "Writings." Out of the 22 books of the Hebrew canon (equivalent to the 39 books of the Protestant Bibles), only 8 are not expressly referred to: Judges, Ruth, Song of Solomon, Ecclesiastes,

Esther, Ezra, Nehemiah, Chronicles. In view of the limited length of most of these books and the nature of their contents, this absence of quotations is in no wise surprising and could hardly be argued to indicate a failure to accept the totality of the Hebrew canon.

On the other hand, it is noteworthy that there is not a single case of definite quotations of any of the books known as Apocrypha and claimed as canonical by the Roman Catholic Church. Inasmuch as a mass of material amounting to almost twenty per cent of the canonical Old Testament is involved it would appear that this absence of reference may scarcely be deemed insignificant.

1. NEW TESTAMENT ATTITUDE TOWARD OLD TESTAMENT SCRIPTURE

Both in the manner in which they are introduced and in the way in which they are used the quotations represent a very impressive witness to the high regard in which the New Testament writings held the Old Testament Scripture.

Formulae of introduction are frequently used to indicate that a quotation is intended. These are quite variegated, ranging from the simple words "and," "it says," "it is written," etc., to much more complex forms in which the human author is named, sometimes with additional data relating to place and circumstance (for instance, Matt. 12:26; Acts 4: 25; 13:33; Rom. 11:2, 4).

Frequently, by the use of words like "say," "swear," "speak," "cry," etc., the formulae bear witness to the fact that the Word of

God addresses us as an oral utterance. Very often also the fact that a written text is in view is marked by the use of words like "Scripture," "it is written," "have ye not read?" etc. In some cases both types of expression are combined as in the formula "the Scripture says" (John 7:38, 42; Rom. 4:3; 9:17; 10:11; 11:2; Gal. 3:8; 4:30; I Tim. 5:18; James 4:5).

Such personification, by which the Scripture is represented as speaking, is carried even further when acts which are in fact God's actions are ascribed to Scripture. Thus in Romans 9:17 we read that, "the scripture saith unto Pharaoh," and the statement quoted is manifestly a statement of God, in which the pronoun "I" refers to God. Similarly, in Galatians 3:8 it is stated that "the scripture, foreseeing that God would justify the heathen through faith, preached before the gospel unto Abraham," and this introduces God's promise to Abraham. As Warfield pointedly noted, "It was not, however, the Scripture (which did not exist at the time) that, foreseeing God's purposes of grace in the future, spoke these precious words to Abraham, but God Himself in His own person: it was not yet existent Scripture that made this announcement to Pharaoh, but God Himself through the mouth of His Prophet Moses. These acts could be attributed to 'Scripture' only as the result of such a habitual identification, in the mind of the writer, of the text of Scripture with God as speaking, that it became natural to use the term 'Scripture says,' when what was really intended was 'God, as recorded in

Scripture, said.' " (*The Inspiration and Authority of the Bible,* S. G. Craig, editor, p. 299f.).

The divine origin of Scripture is prominently featured in the formulae of quotation. In at least fifty-six cases God is explicitly referred to as the author. Among these we may note certain citations in which the text quoted and ascribed to God is not presented in the Old Testament as a direct utterance of God, but rather belongs to the course of the narrative or even is a human statement addressed to God (Matt. 19:5; Acts 4:25; 13:35; Heb. 1:5-8, 13; 3:7; 4:4). Here again we quote Warfield, "It is not God, however, in whose mouth these sayings are placed in the text of the Old Testament: they are the words of others, recorded in the text of Scripture as spoken to or of God. They could be attributed to God only through such habitual identification, in the minds of the writers, of the text of Scripture with the utterances of God that it had become natural to use the term 'God says' when what was really intended was 'Scripture, the Word of God, says' " (*op. cit.,* p. 300).

In some cases the name of the human author of Scripture is given: Moses, David, Isaiah, Jeremiah, Daniel, Joel, Hosea. Many of the passages in which this is the case are, however, references not to personal statements made by these men but rather to divine pronouncements which they were commissioned to transmit and in which the pronoun "I" refers to God. We may take special note of passages where the divine and the human authorship appear together (Matt.

1:22; Mark 12:36; Acts 1:16; 4:25; 28:25; Rom. 9:25). This type of formula bears witness to the fact that in the mind of the New Testament writers the divine superintendence did not obliterate the individual characteristics and personalities of the human authors. Rather they were used in keeping with the divine purpose in terms of their own circumstances, language, and preparation for their holy task and these features are apparent on the record, but they are never construed by the New Testament writers as impinging upon the irrefragable authority and divine authorship of the Scriptures they were commissioned to write.

An added witness to this authority may be found in the way in which the writers of the New Testament, and indeed our Lord himself, appealed to the Scripture with the formula "It is written." This does more than emphasize the fact that a written text is in view, for it implies also an appeal to a final authority from which no exception can be taken. In this same order of thought we notice that occasionally the term "law" is used where reference is made to passages which are not found in the first five books of the Old Testament (John 10:34; 15:25; Rom. 3:19; I Cor. 14:21). These are presented in such a way not as a result of confusion as to the location of these texts in the Old Testament, but because the whole Old Testament was viewed as having legal authority. An interesting parallel may well be found in certain Psalms, such as Psalm 119, where the terminology "law," "statutes," "commandents," etc., may well have a broader reference than the legal portions of the Old Testament. Similarly the term "prophets" may refer to a broader scope of Scripture than that part of the canon designated by that name. An example may be found in Matthew 13:35. This again is due to the fact that for the New Testament writers the whole Old Testament has a prophetic character; it is an address from God and to men mediated by his spokesmen.

Another interesting feature of the formulae of quotations is the frequent use of the present for the introductory words "He says" rather than "He said." This is reinforced by the use of the pronouns "we" and "you" in relation to ancient sayings, "That which was spoken unto you by God" (Matt. 22: 31); "The Holy Spirit also beareth witness to us" (Heb. 10:15; cf. Matt. 15:7; Mark 7:6; 12:19; Acts 4:11; 13:47; Heb. 12:5). In this wise the eternal contemporaneity of Scripture is emphasized, a truth of which explicit expression is found in Romans 15:4, "For whatsoever things were written aforetime were written for our learning" (Note also Rom. 4:23, 24; I Cor. 9:10; 10:11).

Finally it is worthwhile to pause to give attention to the circumstances in which quotations were presented by both our Lord and the apostles. They appeal to Scripture when in debate; they appeal to it when requested to answer questions, whether serious or captious; they appeal to it in connection with their teaching even to those who would not be inclined to press them for other authorities than their own word; they appeal to it to indicate the purpose of some of their own actions or their insight into God's purpose in relation to contemporary developments; and they appeal to it in their prayers. In the case of Jesus, he appealed to it repeatedly in the temptation, where he was facing an adversary who could not be imposed upon in terms of a questionable authority.

Through the whole course of their career we find a consistent note of reverence for and acceptance of the Scripture of the Old Testament as the Word of God. It is not surprising, therefore, that the historic position of the church through the ages has followed very closely their lead in this matter.

2. NEW TESTAMENT INTERPRETATION OF OLD TESTAMENT SCRIPTURE

It would probably be hazardous to assert that the way in which the New Testament interpreted particular passages of the Old Testament was meant to be the norm of all Biblical exegesis. Yet, the example given by the New Testament is a very important clue to a true interpretation of Sacred Scripture.

It is manifest that our Lord and his apostles were viewing the Old Testament Scripture as a text which did not have a merely contemporary and therefore ephemeral significance, but rather as the expression of God's truth, vested with permanent relevancy and capable of direct reference to their own times. They did not, therefore, narrowly confine their interpretation and use of the Old Testament in terms of the immediate historic context in which any particular passage was uttered or written. On the contrary, they saw throughout one pervasive unity of purpose in terms of God's plan which provides for a recurrent relevancy of particular texts. Moreover, in not infrequent cases they deemed that the complete meaning or effectuation of certain Old Testament texts may come to the fore only in the redemptive revelation connected with the incarnation and mediatorial ministry of Jesus Christ. To indicate this relation they used various terms whose exact import deserves to be weighed.

a. *Fulfill* (Matt. 1:22; 5:17, and over thirty times in the New Testament. Cf. also the interesting word *Pleroma* or "fulness," John 1:16; Rom. 13:10). The contrast is not so much "empty" versus "full" as "partially full" versus "more completely full" or even "totally full." This language, therefore, emphasizes that that which was partially disclosed in the Old Testament Scripture and context has now become more fully evident; or again that that which was simply announced in Old Testament times has now become realized in the actuality of history.

b. *Type* (Rom. 5:14; I Cor. 10:6), and *antitype* (Heb. 9:24; I Peter 3:21). Here the emphasis is upon one pattern of truth with various historical manifestations, usually increasingly articulate in their portrayal of the prototype, or ultimate design in the mind of God.

c. *Shadow* (Col. 2:17; Heb. 8:5; 10:1). It is commonly contrasted to substance, although in Hebrews 10:1 the contrasting term is "image." Here the emphasis on the pre-eminence of the New Testament realization is unmistakable.

d. In the same order of thought one might mention some use of the terms *true* or *truth*, especially in the Johannine writings (John 1:17; 6:32; 15:1; etc. Cf. Heb. 8:4), where the implied contrast appears to be with "incomplete" or "partial disclosure" rather than with "falsehood."

It is within this general framework of reference that the New Testament interpretation of the Old Testament finds its place. In spite of a few difficult passages, it has been widely acknowledged that the New Testament offers a strikingly illuminating interpretation of the Old. C. H. Dodd states, "It must be conceded that we have before us a considerable intellectual feat. The various scriptures are acutely interpreted along lines already discernible within the Old Testament canon itself or in pre-Christian Judaism — in many cases, I believe, lines which start from their first, historical, intention — and these lines are carried forward to fresh results. Very diverse scriptures are brought together so that they interpret one another in hitherto unsuspected ways" (*According to the Scriptures,* p. 109).

Even passages which have frequently been viewed as difficult, and sometimes advanced as examples of farfetched and artificial exegesis, may well receive an appropriate explanation in terms of this total understanding of the divine purpose and of the pneumatic unity of the Scriptures. For instance, Matthew 2:15 applies to Christ the statement of Hosea 11:1, "Out of Egypt have I called my son," which in the original context has surely a primary reference to the Exodus in the time of Moses. Matthew, however, far from making an artificial and illegitimate transference of the text to Christ, simply views Moses' exodus as one element in the great redemptive pattern which runs through history, an element which bears a striking resemblance, even geographically, to certain features of the career of Jesus Christ the Messiah, through whom redemption was to be accomplished and the spiritual exodus of God's people effected. It is worthwhile to read Patrick Fairbairn's eloquent pages on this subject (*Typology of Scripture,* 6th. ed., Vol. I., p. 450 ff. Also in Zondervan reprint).

While an acknowledgement of the pneumatic unity of Scripture and of the overarching redemptive purpose of God (*Heilsgeschichte*) will greatly assist in gaining a proper understanding of passages that were sometimes alleged to be strained, it is not claimed here that this principle will automatically resolve all the difficulties that may be encountered in this area. It may be wise to keep in mind the following considerations.

a. It is not necessary to assume in every case that the Old Testament writers or their immediate audience had a clear grasp of the full scope of meaning of their pronouncement, nor specifically of its fulfillment in New Testament times. The Holy Spirit of God who inspired them may well have led them to say things which had a certain relationship to their contemporary situation, to be sure, but whose ultimate God-breathed meaning far surpassed what was immediately understood or intended. This was surely the case for Caiaphas (John 11:49-52), and it may well have occurred to a greater or lesser degree in connection with certain Old Testament Scriptures.

b. Evangelicals naturally hold that any New Testament interpretation of an Old Testament text is legitimate. They do not feel bound to assert that it is necessarily exclusive or exhaustive of the full Old Testament meaning. Certain Old Testament passages may have conveyed to the original hearers a more restricted sense than the perspective that is presented in the New Testament. The original understanding was a legitimate interpretation which is now supplemented, not cancelled, by the larger vistas of the New Testament, and which in turn does not preclude the propriety of these larger vistas, now authoritatively revealed in the New Testament.

c. It may be wise to remember that the New Testament authors were so immersed in the language and the thought patterns of the Old Testament that expressions which are drawn from it seem to come naturally to their lips or to their pen. Some people versed in a certain favorite author, like Shakespeare, frequently do express themselves in forms of language derived from his writings, without thereby meaning to suggest a complete situational correspondance. Similarly, the fact that Old Testament phrases are used does not necessarily imply that the New Testament author asserted a direct relationship between the original passage and the New Testament context. Sometimes such a relationship is explicitly asserted, but when it is not, we are not in a position to say that it is implied in the presence of verbal resemblances.

d. The New Testament authors at times amalgamate various Old Testament passages in such a way that these supplement each other and are brought into illuminating focus in terms of the New Testament situation. A good example of this procedure may be found in II Corinthians 6:16-18, in which we find a composite of references to Ezekiel 37:27; Leviticus 26:11, 12; Isaiah 52:11, 12; Ezekiel 20:34; and II Samuel 7:14.

e. The New Testament writers apparently did not hesitate in a number of cases to modify the wording of the Old Testament, or even to introduce comments of their own in order to indicate in what way they construed or applied the Old Testament text. Ephesians 6:2, 3 provides an example of this practice. Occasionally it is not easy to determine what was intended as commentary and what was meant as quotation. The whole question of the verbal accuracy of the New Testament quotations is too complex to be discussed here. For a very brief treatment of it we may perhaps be permitted to refer the reader to what we have written elsewhere in an article, "New Testament Use of the Old Testament" in *Revelation and the Bible* (Carl F. H. Henry, ed.; Grand Rapids, 1958, pp. 135-151).

BIBLIOGRAPHY

Dittmar, Wilhelm, *Vetus Testamentum in Novo*. Goettingen, 1903.

Dodd, C. H., *According to the Scriptures*. London, 1952.

Ellis, E. E., *Paul's Use of the Old Testament*. Grand Rapids, 1957.

Fairbairn, Patrick, *Hermeneutical Manual,* pp. 354-460. Edinburgh, 1858.

Lindars, Barnabas, *New Testament Apologeic: The Doctrinal Significance of Old Testament Quotations*. Philadelphia, 1961.

Mickelsen, A. B., *Interpreting the Bible*. Grand Rapids, 1963.

Sweet, L. M., "Quotations," *ISBE*.

Turpie, D. M., *The Old Testament in the New*. London, 1868.

4

The Use of Archaeology in Interpretation

Viewed historically the Bible is a valuable collection of ancient documents, covering, if it may be assumed that written records dating back to Abraham found incorporation in the Pentateuch, something like 2000 years of history and literary activity. It is the first task of the interpreter to determine what the writer of any given work of literature, or record of history, originally intended to communicate. For that reason all information which elucidates his language, throws light on his social context, explains allusions, or otherwise provides contemporary comment on his meaning, the understanding and outlook of his public, and his own plan and purpose, is an aid to exegesis. The sources of such information are largely archaeological in the case of the Old Testament. The New Testament, which classical historians have too commonly disregarded as an important document of first century history and the Roman peace, is contemporary with the written records of sophisticated literary societies, and is less dependent for its interpretation on the diligence of archaeological research. It is, nonetheless, richly illuminated by it, in common with the secular history of a fairly well-documented age. Surviving non-Biblical literary documents from the civilizations of the Fertile Crescent, epigraphical records of five empires, works of art, and a thousand lesser and more elusive memorials of human activity, artifacts. papyri, potsherds, and the indelible marks of man's work and worship, are all relevant material for the interpretation of the Bible.

Archaeology, in its varied forms of activity, has provided most of this material. Thanks to its skilled and scientific application it is possible today to understand the Bible in its setting of time and place as never before. To grasp with clarity the writer's first meaning and original purpose is manifestly the first step towards the elucidation of that which is permanent and universally significant in his theme. Such understanding is logically the interpreter's first task, and archaeology in its breadth and achievement ment. This article is not a survey of Biblical archaeology in its breadth and achievement A number of competent works deal adequately with the subject as a whole. It is the present object to suggest the preacher's and teacher's approach to archaeology as an aid to exegesis. Illustration under four heads will be the most effective demonstration.

1. ARCHAEOLOGICAL MATERIAL WHICH ELUCIDATES BACKGROUND AND CONTEXT

The events of the Bible did not take place in a vacuum. They were part of ancient history. The theme of the Bible is that stream of human faith, action, and endeavor which found consummation in the New Testament. The actors, nevertheless, moved on a stage which is becoming wider, deeper, and clearer in the light of archaeological discovery. In the past, the view was held that the stories of the patriarchs were folk-tales of the sort which gather round the origins of a people and were of no historical worth. Abraham was of no more significance than Aeneas, unearthed by Greeks of Magna Graecia from a motley stock of Trojan legend, as a canny compliment to emerging Rome. It is no longer possible to hold that view. Ur of the Chaldees was first shown by Leonard Woolley to be a mature and literary society, but Ur was only one place, and her history only one chapter, of the crowded story of the Euphrates valley. Movement and migration had taken place from time immemorial round what Henry Breasted called the Fertile Crescent, and Abraham's wanderings were part of a process repeated more than once in the story of the river civilizations of the Near and Middle East. By the same path came Canaanite and Phoenician in unrecorded folk migrations.

The unique feature of Abraham's story is the wealth of detail which accompanies it in the fine literary accounts in Genesis. It is almost possible to pick the point where the laborious brevity of the clay tablet was succeeded by the more roomy and ample style which the papyrus made possible and to assess the early documents which Abraham no doubt bequeathed to his family and Moses' later editing. In accordance with ancient custom his own family must have kept a record. Truth and authenticity are embedded in detail, and it is there that the investigator must look in measuring the historical value of a story. The laws, literature, and business documents of the Euphrates valley have provided a wealth of comment on the stories of the patriarchs but comment may be confined to the striking documents from Nuzi. The Hurrians of the Nuzi texts were well-acquainted with the Habiru of the Amarna letters and the Ras Shamra tablets, and demonstrate a community of custom with the Hebrew patriarchs which goes far to support the contention that Habiru and Hebrew were the same. Sarah's search for an heir by means of her maid Hagar, her legal casting out of Hagar on Isaac's birth, Abraham's adoption of Eliezer as his heir, Esau's contemptuous sale of his birthright, Laban's and Jacob's partnership, Rachel's attempt to confirm succession by the theft of the teraphim, and Isaac's irrevocable bestowal of the blessing all find detailed parallel in the Nuzi tablets. The stories of the patriarchs are obviously authentic history, and to be interpreted as such. Genesis is vindicated as a reliable record, and interpretation can proceed with the added certainty that those who move through its pages were real people and not the figures of legend or saga.

Qumran provides a parallel illustration for the New Testament. The abiding worth of the now famous Dead Sea Scrolls for the New Testament scholar is probably the light which they throw on the "third force" in Palestine, "the Remnant" of the true and faithful, distinct from the organized groupings of Sadducee and Pharisee, in revolt against urban religion, and hitherto visible only in the New Testament. Of such were the more obscure figures of the Gospels, the fishermen of Galilee, the "common people" who "heard him gladly," the followers of John, the parents of John, Mary herself, the Bethany household, and the widow with the mite. The scrolls from the caves have demonstrated the reality of this social and religious substratum. Like masses of nonliterary papyri from Egypt, the Qumran documents show the realities of common life, and the earthy truth of the New Testament. They underline the fact that the Gospels are a document of first century history, giving what no other literary record gives in such volume, a glimpse of the proletariat and life as it was lived by common folk in Rome's most uneasy and turbulent province.

The lesson for the interpreter again emerges. Any theory of literary origins which treats the four Gospels as other than a plain record put together by eyewitnesses, must be forthwith suspect in the light of the social evidence from papyrological sources. Interpretation can begin with one advantage if it can stand on such evidence in the face of the sharp attacks of the critics.

Another lesson takes shape from the examination of the archaeological material, and that is the unique ethical and monotheistic emphasis of the Bible. Sumeria, Babylon, and Assyria have provided in their surviving literature accounts of creation, man's innocence and fall, and the judgment

58

of a deluge. Babylon, the Hittites, and other smaller communities, provide examples of codes of law. The interpreter and apologist has only to set this parallel, earlier, and contemporary material side by side with the Biblical documents to demonstrate that the Hebrew stood apart, reserved, free from the crudities of the pagan mythologies, related to a theme and an unfolding purpose, lofty in ethics, and austerely monotheistic. If the Bible does not invent, it appropriates, adapts, and transforms. Phrases from the Lord's prayer are to be found in rabbinical liturgies. The theological language of Paul is sometimes that of the mystery cults, Christmas was Mithras' birthday, etc. Of what significance are these facts? Simply that the divine method, here as with the personality of man, is not obliteration but sublimation, and the transformation of that which is committed.

2. ARCHAEOLOGICAL MATERIAL OF APOLOGETIC VALUE

This aspect of interpretation has been touched upon above. The era of modern archaeology burst on the world with high drama, both in the classical and Biblical spheres. Schliemann discovered Troy and Mycenae, and demonstrated the absurdity of the corrupted interpretation of the Greek epics, Aegean history, and the mythology of the Mediterranean cultures. The lesson was repeated as civilization after civilization was unearthed — the Assyrians, the Babylonians, the Hittites, the Cretans. Layard preceded Schliemann with the recovery of Nineveh; Woolley succeeded him in the excavation of Ur. A dozen great names will always be listed as the pioneers of an astonishing era of discovery which thrust back the frontiers of history for scores of centuries, and so frequently demonstrated the truth and reliability of tradition that Biblical scholars of the conservative school and Christian apologists took to quoting the work of the archaeologists with something like triumph. There is no doubt that some of this enthusiasm was justified. Confirmation of otherwise unsupported detail in the Biblical records by the documents from the Euphrates valley and Assyria, or by the epigraphical evidence of Asia Minor and of Greece, has been a constant encouragement to those who rightly see a firm foundation for Christian doctrine in the reliability and authority of the Bible. The life story and research of Sir William Ramsay, the classical and Biblical scholar in Asia Minor is striking illustration of the process by which more than one honest mind returned to a confidence in the Scriptural records from the synthetic skepticism of nineteenth century scholarship Particular illustration is found in the complete vindication of Luke as an historian, the justification of his language, and the confirmation of his casual detail. The Nazareth Decree, with its strange light on the Pharisaic account of the empty tomb is a more recent illustration (see the present writer's *Out of the Earth*, chap. 4).

Thanks to archaeology, the interpreter can turn to Scripture with a much greater confidence in the historical worth of the documents and can dismiss with firmness the neo-liberal approach which, under varied forms of "demythologizing," is paradoxically creating a new mythology. So often has the hasty assumption, and the far fetched theory, crumbled at the touch of the archaeological discovery that informed conservatism can await with some tranquillity the passing of the ephemeral fashions of the liberal school. The collapse of the assumptions of the Tubingen School on the question of the Fourth Gospel is now history, and the recovery of Tatian's Diatesseron on which a galleon of theory was wrecked, can hardly be classified as an archaeological achievement. The papyrus fragment in the Manchester University library which takes the dating of John back to A.D. 125 can, however, be regarded as an archaeological prize, and the whole story illustrates the contention set forth above. The apologetic value of archaeology to the orthodox and conservative interpreter must be ranked highly.

3. ARCHAEOLOGICAL MATERIAL OF ARTISTIC SIGNIFICANCE

Art is both a rendering and a representation of life. The realism of mural art in Egypt and Assyria is a strong light upon society and human action in many spheres. Greek vase paintings have illustrated and explained more than one obscure corner in the interpretation of the classics; and if the exegesis of the Bible has less instances of such aid to quote, the help of such representational art has nevertheless deepened understanding. Professor Yigael Yadin's sumptuously illustrated book on warfare in Biblical times demonstrates the importance of surviving samples of weaponry and surviving artwork representations of battles, sieges, and all manner of military activity for the interpretation of ancient history.

Nor is war the only sphere where archaeology similarly elucidates a Biblical context or reinforces a critical argument. Early use of the vine and branches in Christian decorative art adds weight to the argument for an early date for the fourth Gospel. And consider the throne-like altar to Zeus from Pergamum, set up today in the East Berlin Museum. It throws considerable light on the symbolism of the apocalyptic letter to Pergamum, whose church dwelt "where Satan's seat is" (Rev. 2:13). The altar somehow summed up the pervasive paganism of the place with its worship of the imperial cult, and its devotion to the serpent-ridden Asklepios. Ramsay's book on the *Letters to the Seven Churches of Asia,* a landmark in the interpretation of the elusive imagery of the Apocalypse, draws heavily on art and architecture, no less than on the artistry of coinage, for the writer's convincing elucidations.

Illustration is widespread. An ear of corn, carved on a fallen plinth in the precinct of Demeter at Eleusis, near Athens, is a reference to the symbolic significance of the uplifted ear of corn in the mystery cult once celebrated here, and considerable light on the image of the corn of wheat which Christ expounded to a group of Greeks. Since Paul must have passed through Eleusis on his way to Corinth, it is significant too that the illustration of the dying grain recurs in his epistle to Corinth. And Paul's amaing Areopagus address is illuminated by reference to the artistic wonders on the rocky platform of the Acropolis above where he spoke, but whose relevance in the quest for truth were quickly dismissed.

4. ARCHAEOLOGICAL MATERIAL OF LITERARY SIGNIFICANCE

Much of the material which might have been assembled here has found a place under other headings above. The significance of the cuneiform records of Assyria and the Euphrates valley for the interpretation of the early chapters of Genesis has already been discussed. Of equal relevance is Egyptian literature, also the gift of archaeology. A. S Yahauda showed from this source, many years ago, how unerringly accurate in detail, background, and atmosphere were the closing chapters of Genesis and the early chapters of Exodus. Akhnaton's *Hymn to the Sun*, and similar surviving poetry, demonstrates the poetic psalm in a non-Biblical context, and reveals that the Hebrew psalter was in the full stream of ancient lyrism.

The nonliterary papyri, recovered in vast numbers from the sites of ancient towns south of the rain-line in Egypt, have shed floods of light on the New Testament. The human situation envisaged in the parables of Christ can be illustrated again and again from this correspondence in a manner which emphasizes the realism and contemporary relevance of Christ's teaching and the authenticity of the documents which record it. The form of the ancient letter with its opening formalities, its body of information and request, and its personal greetings at the end is similar comment on the epistles of the New Testament. It was Adolf Deissmann, a young German scholar, who first drew attention to the worth and significance of the papyri in this regard, at the end of the nineteenth century. His *Licht vom Osten* was another landmark in New Testament studies.

5. ARCHAEOLOGICAL MATERIAL OF LINGUISTIC SIGNIFICANCE

It was part of Deissmann's thesis that the Greek of the nonliterary papyri, the common spoken Greek of everyday intercourse, was also the Greek of the New Testament. The language of the papyri has thrown light on many difficult contexts in the New Testament. Examples are too numerous to quote, but the discovery that *meris* meant "a region" set Luke's description of Philippi in its correct geographical light. If *hypostasis* means "title-deeds" as well as "substance," a vivid interpretation of Hebrews 11:1 is made possible. Since *apecho* can be shown to provide a formula for a receipt, quaint light is thrown on the use of the word by Matthew, the tax collector, in the context which dismisses the Pharisaic exhibitionists as already "paid in full." If *epiousion* can refer to the day which is beginning, and has shed its classical meaning of "tomorrow," a difficult phrase in the Lord's Prayer is cleared up. It is the meaning of the word in common parlance which is so often relevant to the correct understanding of a text, and archaeology has provided the raw linguistic material for this.

The Dead Sea Scrolls share this exegetical importance with the Egyptian papyri. The ancient texts which the scrolls provide have cleared up the numerical contradiction between Exodus 1:5 and Acts 7:14 by supporting with a contemporary text the reading followed in Acts and in the Greek Septuagint. They have proved that Hebrews 1:6 is, in fact, a quotation from Deuteronomy 32:43. The magnificent scroll of Isaiah has cleared up difficulties in 3:24; 20:1, 8; and 49:12. The teaching of the Qumran sect illustrates twice the Sermon on the Mount. The Lord directly rebukes their doctrine in Matthew 5:43, and approves it in Matthew 18:15-17. The same texts show that "the poor in spirit" means "the tender-hearted."

In conclusion let it again be stressed that all competent interpretation must begin with the basic and contemporary meaning of a document. If that is not plain, the secondary and more general meaning is likely to prove elusive. The present object has been to show that archaeology, by its recovery and description of the context and background — social, political, topical, literary, linguistic, historical, and geographical, can frequently elucidate and illuminate dark corners in a manner which the interpreter cannot well neglect. His study of the archaeological evidence is therefore of prime concern.

BIBLIOGRAPHY

Banks, F. A., *Coins of Bible Days*. Macmillan.

Boulton, W. H., *Archaeology Explains*. Epworth Press.

Blaiklock, E. M., *Out of the Earth*. Paternoster.

Bruce, F. F., *Second Thoughts on the Dead Sea Scrolls*. Paternoster.

Coburn, C. M., *The New Archaeological Discoveries*. Funk and Wagnalls.

Eisenberg, A., and Elkins, D. P., *Worlds Lost and Found*. Abelard Sherman.

Harrison, R. K., *A History of Old Testament Times*. Zondervan.

Kitchen, J. H., *Holy Fields*. Eerdmans.

Pfeiffer, C. F., *The Biblical World*. Baker Book House.

Ramsay, W. M., *Letters to the Seven Churches*. Hodder and Stoughton. Reprint 1963 by Baker Book House.

Thompson, J. A., *The Bible and Archaeology*. Eerdmans.

Unger, M. F., *Archaeology and the Old Testament*. Zondervan.

Wiseman, D. J., *Illustrations from Biblical Archaeology*. Tyndale Press.

5

The Dead Sea Scrolls and Interpretation

The chance discovery in 1947 of some ancient scrolls, cached in a cave near the northwestern shore of the Dead Sea, began an amazing, and ever-growing, series of archaeological expeditions and scholarly researches. Thousands of pieces of Biblical, apocryphal, and sectarian manuscripts have come to light, which have affected the interpretation of the Bible. For our purposes here, only the texts from Qumran (the area of the original finds, seven miles south of Jericho) are relevant.

1. THE RELATIONSHIP TO THE BIBLICAL TEXT

The starting point of interpretation is the establishment of the "original" text, for it is well known that the text of the Bible has not been transmitted to us free from all scribal defect. This does not mean that matters of basic doctrine are in question, but rather that the text of the Bible has various obscure and unintelligible passages. But into the midst of this difficulty the texts from Qumran have come as a tremendous help, primarily for the Old Testament, for no New Testament materials were found at this site.

a. New materials. The method by which scholars seek to resolve the difficulties of the text in order to begin interpretation is called "textual criticism." The task is carried on by three primary means: (a) comparing different manuscripts, noting their agreements and differences, and arriving at an eclectic, and what is believed original, text; (b) comparing Hebrew manuscripts with ancient versions, because these translations are often based on earlier Hebrew manuscripts than have been preserved; and (c) conjectural emendation, that is, scholarly conjecture as to the original text, based on knowledge of the ways errors may occur in transcribing manuscripts. Obviously the best means is the comparison of manuscripts. However, prior to the discovery of the Scrolls this was not possible in the Old Testament on any large scale. Because of the Jewish practice of discarding and eventually burying old manuscripts, and because of persecutions and other reasons, no manuscripts (except for a few fragments) of the Old Testament earlier than the ninth and tenth centuries A.D. have survived.

Another problem has been the fact that all these medieval manuscripts agree very closely with one another, except in minor orthographic matters. The reason for this is that all medieval Hebrew manuscripts in the dominant tradition have descended from a common ancestor or single scroll. Around A.D. 100, as a result primarily of the council of Jamnia and the labors of rabbi Aqiba, a standardized, authoritative text was established out of the various textual traditions in the pre-Christian period. All variant lines of tradition were destroyed, or at least were brought into agreement with the *textus receptus*. The result was that from then on all manuscripts were made on the basis of this one authoritative text. And this is what has come to be known as the Masoretic text.

The discovery of the Qumran scrolls breached this barrier of A.D. 100. Now, for the first time, we can get a firsthand look at the state of the Old Testament text in Christian times. The Qumran texts date just prior to the stabilization of the consonantal text in A.D. 100, that is, about the second to the first century B.C.

b. New value judgments. In the process of comparing different manuscripts of the Bible with ancient versions in order to determine the correct reading for interpretation, it is necessary to have some understanding of the trustworthiness of these versions. The study of the Scrolls has brought a new appreciation of the value of certain versional evidence. Research has shown that in the days of the Qumran scribes there were at least three different textual traditions in common circulation. In other words, the texts found at Qumran fall into three separate "families" or traditions regarding the state of the text. Many of them are very similar to the Masoretic text, and so indicate that they are the tradition which was eventually accepted and standardized in A.D. 100. Others, however, agree closely with the readings in the Septuagint (the Greek version translated between 250 and 100 B.C.), and thus show that they are in a line with the Hebrew text upon which it was based. Yet some scrolls agree with neither, and on various occasions show affinities with the Samaritan Pentateuch (the Hebrew text copied by the Samaritans after the schism in the middle of the fourth century B.C.).

What all this indicates is that in the centuries before Christ there was not just one authoritative text. Various traditions were accepted and used. This means that from now on textual criticism must not be content with using the evidence of the Septuagint or Samaritan Pentateuch as a last resort. It must, rather, give greater weight to variant textual traditions reflected in these sources.

c. New clarifications. The manuscripts from Qumran and the new appreciation of the versions have yielded information that clarifies many individual texts, particularly in the Old Testament. A few examples will illustrate this.

The Old Testament committee of the Revised Standard Version had access to the complete scroll of Isaiah (IQIs[a]) found in the first cave. It eventually decided to adopt thirteen readings in the scroll that differed from the Masoretic text. Each has been marked in the margin with the note "one ancient Ms." For example, the Masoretic text of Isaiah 21:8 reads, as translated in the KJV, "And he cried, A lion." But this does not fit the context, for the immediately preceding verses speak of the watchman seeing horsemen, asses, and camels, not a lion. The ASV, sensing this difficulty, translates,

"And he cried as a lion," but this is not what the text says. The Qumran scroll of Isaiah has at this point, "then he who saw cried," as the RSV reads. The difference between the words "a lion" and "he who saw" involves basically the interchange of two consonants in Hebrew, probably a scribal error caused by confusing sounds as a text was being dictated for copying. The Qumran scroll clearly makes better sense.

In the Masoretic text of I Samuel 23:11-12 David asks two questions, and the Lord answers only the second one. David then in verse twelve repeats his first question, and finally gets an answer. The Septuagint, however, omits both the second question and the Lord's answer to the first one. The Qumran scroll (4QSam^b) has apparently preserved the original text, for it separates the two questions and gives an answer to each, "But now, will Saul go down, as your servant has heard? O Lord God of Israel, tell your servant. And the Lord said, He will go down. Then David asked, Will the men of Keilah hand me and my men over to Saul? They will deliver you, replied the Lord."

In Hebrews 1:6 there is quoted, supposedly from the Old Testament, the phrase, "let all the angels of God worship him." But this cannot be found in the Masoretic text. However, a fragment of Deuteronomy 32(4Q Deut 32) found at Qumran contains this extra phrase. It reads, "bow down (worship) to him, all ye gods." The Septuagint (which the author of Hebrews was quoting) also contains this line, and the evidence from Qumran suggests this was original.

One should remember in all this that because a reading appears in the Qumran Scrolls does not mean it is automatically to be preferred. Habakkuk 2:15 is a case in point. In the Masoretic text we read the phrase "gaze on their nakedness," but the Qumran commentary on Habakkuk reads "gaze on their feasts." The two words "nakedness" and "feasts" are very similar in Hebrew, the only difference being one letter. But there seems to be no reason to change the Masoretic text, since the Qumran reading appears to be a deliberate change motivated by interpretational purposes. The commentary that follows this passage stresses that a certain evil event took place on the Day of Atonement, that is, on a "feast" day!

2. THE RELATIONSHIP TO BIBLICAL TERMINOLOGY AND THOUGHT

Many times the problem of interpretation rests not with a corrupt text, but rather with an obscure terminology. Biblical languages have not been spoken for 2000 years, and thus word and phrase meanings have often become lost. Or it may be that a word occurs only once or twice in the Bible, and so does not provide sufficient contexts in which to clarify its meaning. The Scrolls provide many more contexts against which to interpret the signiificance of Biblical terminology. Only a few examples will be given here.

a. *The Old Testament.* In Micah 6:8 occur the familiar ords, "to do justice, and to love kindness, and to walk humbly with your God" (RSV). All of the major English versions translate this phrase in a similar fashion. But it is possible to translate the Hebrew text somewhat differently: "to practice justice and love of kindness, and to walk humbly with your God." In this case "love of kindness" would be the object of "practice." The problem, of course, centers on the word "love," which in Hebrew can be read either as an infinitive "to love" or as a noun "love." Which is correct? Here the Scrolls come as a help. W. Brownlee in *The Meaning of the Qumran Scrolls for the Bible* (p. 108), has pointed out that in the Manual of Discipline 2:24-25 there is an allusion to Micah 6:8 in the sentence, "for they shall all live in unity of truth, and humility of goodness, and love of kindness, and purpose of righteousness." This series of constructs, because of the particular words used, suggests that this means "true unity and good humility and kindly love and righteous purpose." That this is correct is given confirmation by another passage in the Manual, namely, 8:1-2: "in the council of the community there shall be twelve laymen and three priests, who are perfect in all that has been revealed of the whole law, who shall practice truth and righteousness and kindly love [love of kindness], who shall walk humbly a man with his neighbor." The point of all this is that the Scrolls show clearly that the word "love" in Micah 6:8 is not an infinitive, but rather a noun with a qualifying attribute "kindly," or better (as the word "kindly" in Hebrew combines the ideas of love and loyalty) "devoted." Thus

Micah 6:8 should be translated,

"He has showed you, O man, what is good;
    and what does the Lord require of you
but to practice justice and devoted love,
    and to walk humbly with your God."

The whole passage would then reflect the twofold path of godly living stressed in Deuteronomy 6:5 and Leviticus 19:18 (cf. Mark. 12:28-31).

The Qumran sect, however, does not always give us such clarification. It had its own method of Biblical interpretation, which shows the dangers of a predetermined point of view on the meaning of the text. The sect interpreted the Old Testament against the background of its own belief that it was living in the last days, and thus discovered, so it believed, that the prophets had prophesied almost exclusively of those days. Therefore, by allegory and variant reading and words out of context, the sect found guidance in the prophets for the last, difficult times in which they lived. A commentary on Micah from cave 1 is a good example. In Micah 1:5 we find the words, "all this is for the transgression of Jacob, and for the sins of the house of Israel. What is the transgression of Jacob? Is it not Samaria? And what is the sin of the house of Jacob? Is it not Jerusalem?" (RSV). The RSV has followed the Septuagint in reading the phrase "the sin of the house of Judah," but the Masoretic text reads "the high places of Judah"; the Micah commentary agrees with the Masoretic text, except in reading the singular "high place." But, in any case, as the context shows, the reference is to the idolatrous worship found in the capital cities of Samaria and Jerusalem. However, at Qumran, "the transgression of Jacob" was interpreted as referring to "the prophet of lies, who leads the simple astray." And "the high place of Judah" is seen as a reference to the "Teacher of Righteousness," the one who led and interpreted the law to the sect. The "prophet of lies," as other contexts indicate, was probably the leader of a rival group, perhaps of the Pharisees. Here, then, allegory has taken the place of contextual exegesis.

b. *The New Testament.* In Luke 2:14, as is usually translated, the angels sang in praise to God: "Glory to God in the highest and on earth peace, good will towards men." This is now seen to have been incorrectly translated, as the RSV reflects. The Greek word *eudokia*, usually "good will," is the equivalent of the Hebrew *ratson*, a term which occurs on various occasions in the Scrolls. But at Qumran it usually carried a special connotation, namely, "God's grace" or "God's good will." Thus in the Hymns of Thanksgiving, in a passage very reminiscent of Luke 2:14, it says that God desires men to know "the abundance of his mercies towards all the sons of his grace [*ratson*]" (4:33). Or in 11:9 the author sings that "thy mercy is towards the sons of thy goodwill." And, conversely, the writer of 10:5-6 admits that the person without this *ratson* is nothing: "I am dust and ashes. What can I devise, if thou art unwilling, and what can I contrive, apart from thy grace [*ratson*]" All this suggests that during the days of the New Testament the term *ratson*, in the kind of context found in Luke 2:14, carried the idea of "divine good pleasure." Thus the passage should be translated, "Glory to God in the highest, and on earth peace to men of God's grace." The promise is that those who know God's good pleasure, and live in it, shall have peace.

3. THE RELATIONSHIP TO CHRISTIANITY

More controversial than individual passages has been the discussion over the significance of the Scrolls for the uniqueness of Christianity. Some have taken up the old position of E. Renan that Christianity is only another form of Essenism which happened to succeed, and have sought to buttress this argument by showing that for its ideas and practices the New Testament was dependent on the Qumran community of Essenes. However, although there are many striking similarities, there are also basic differences which clearly separate the two communities.

The Gospel of John is largely constructed on the theme of the conflict between light and darkness. So John 1:4-5 reads, "In him was life, and the life was the light of men. The light shines in the darkness, and the darkness has not overcome it" (RSV). This same theme is basic to the Scrolls. We learn from the Manual of Discipline that the world is ruled by two powers, one good and one evil, both of them having been created by God (1QS 3:25). The good power is termed the "spirit of truth" or the "prince of lights" (1QS 3:18-24), while the evil force is called the "spirit of perversity" or the "angel of darkness" (1QS 3:19-21). According to Qumran thought all members of the sect were "children of light" (1QS 1:9), a designation also given to Christians in John 12:36, while all outside the group were "children of darkness" (1QS 1:10). The Gospel of John also knows of those who walk in darkness (12:35).

But we should not confuse this "dualism" of Qumran and John. They are both simply using common terminology which was well-known to their contemporaries. What is important is the meaning of the terms. At Qumran a person became a "son of light" by joining the community and obeying its strict interpretation of the Law. In John one becomes a "son of light" by faith in Christ, who himself is the light of the world (cf. John 12:36, 46). Perhaps John is addressing himself to those who had become enamored with Essene thought, and thus radically alters its content. In any case, the Scrolls show that the background of the terminology is thoroughly Jewish, and not Hellenistic (as claimed by Dodd), or Gnostic (as suggested by Bultmann).

Many have thought that in practice, as well as in terminology, there was a link between Qumran and the church. For example, the baptismal practices of Qumran are sometimes thought to be the source of Christian baptism. But at Qumran baptismal practice included daily ablutions for ritual purity, initiatory ablutions for probationary members, and annual ablutions for covenant renewal. The only similarity to some Christian usage is the mode of immersion, and the fact that it was accompanied by repentance, a slim base upon which to build a theory of dependence. The same is true of the sect's "sacred meal." In the Messianic Rule (1QSa) directions are given for a meal consisting of bread and wine, over which prayers are said by the presiding priest. Although some would see here the background to the Christian Eucharist, nowhere is anything said about a sacramental character to the meal, nor of it being a memorial.

Much has also been made of possible relationships between Qumran and John the Baptist and Jesus. As to John the Baptist, there are many possible links with the Qumran sect. He began his ministry near the site of Qumran (Luke 1:80); he was from a priestly background (Luke 1:8-9) that would have found acceptance in the priestly-run sect of Qumran, whose members called themselves the "sons of Zadok" (1QS 8:4-10); he stressed the importance of baptism being accompanied by repentance, as did Qumran (Luke 3:7-9; 1QS 3:6-11); and he found the basis of his ministry in Isaiah 40:3, the foundation text at Qumran (John 1:23; 1QS 8:13-15). It is possible, in light of this, that John may have belonged to the community for a time; at least he probably knew something about their thought and way of life. But John's basic ministry was entirely independent of Qumran, and, indeed, quite opposed to it. John's ministry was essentially prophetic; the sect's was esoteric. John issued a public call to repentance; the sect withdrew to the desert. John's message was free of the legal emphasis found at Qumran. John invited all to repent, while the Qumran community hated its enemies. John baptized once all who repented; Qumran repeated the rite.

The relationship between Jesus and the Qumran leader — the Teacher of Righteousness — is another matter. There is no reason to suspect any link at all. John at least was an ascetic, but Jesus was not (cf. Matt. 11: 19). Before his public ministry Jesus did not live in the wilderness; it was only during his forty days of temptation that he was there, and this would not provide much opportunity for learning the wisdom of Qumran, particularly since Mark says he was with "the wild beasts" (Mark 1:13). Although there are clear parallels between the teachings of Qumran and of Jesus (cf. Matt. 18: 15-17 and IQS 5:24-6:1), there are also striking differences, particularly in relation to the authority of the Law (cf. the constant "but I say unto you" in the Sermon on the Mount). And there is little about the lives of Jesus and the Teacher of Righteousness that is similar. The latter was not crucified, had no saving efficacy attached to his death, and was not expected to rise from the dead.

The conclusion to all this is that, first, the similarities do not suggest any immediate relationship between the Scrolls and the New Testament. Rather, they indicate simply that Jesus and the disciples used the vocabulary of their contemporaries. Jesus did not appear in an historical vacuum. He did not come speaking of things about which men had never thought, nor using a heavenly language. And, secondly, the differences indicate a tremendous gap between Qumran thought and Christian belief. The central figure in this difference is Jesus Christ; there was no one like him at Qumran. The Scrolls do not destroy the uniqueness of Christianity, nor confirm any doctrine.

BIBLIOGRAPHY

Brownlee, W., *The Meaning of the Qumran Scrolls for the Bible*. New York: Oxford, 1964.

Burrows, M., *The Dead Sea Scrolls*. New York: Viking, 1955.

————————, *More Light on the Dead Sea Scrolls*. New York: Viking, 1958.

Cross, F., *The Ancient Library of Qumran and Modern Biblical Studies*. Garden City: Doubleday, 1958.

Ringgren, H., *The Faith of Qumran*. Philadelphia: Fortress, 1963.

Vermes, G., *The Dead Sea Scrolls in English*. Baltimore: Penguin, 1962.

6

Reformation Interpretation
(1457-1560)

For a thousand years Pope Gregory I
(A.D. 590-504) dominated Latin Biblical
interpretation. His commentary on Job set
forth a rich homiletical harvest for the medieval world. By the year A.D. 800 Augustine,
Jerome, Ambrose, and Gregory controlled
early medieval Biblical exegesis. The loss of
Greek and the logic of scholasticism ossified
Biblical study until the marriage between
homiletics and fourteenth century scholarship
buried the text beyond recognition. But the
men of the Reformation restored to the church
sound Biblical interpretation.

1. A HUMANIST HERMENEUTIC

In March of 1457 Laurentius Valla at-
tacked Aquinas as an interpreter, preferring
Paul as a theologian. When in his notes on
the New Testament Valla turned to the Greek
text, a positive reform of theology began.
Careful attention to that text would remove
"the clamor of strangers in the presence of
God's Word, for His Word is our life." Erasmus discovered Valla's notes in the Parc
monastery, publishing them in 1505. Bade
wrote in his preface to that edition, "Valla
has deserved the greatest favour and grati-

tude of every studious man." Erasmus earned the gratitude of all the reformers for his 1516 edition of the Greek New Testament with its fresh Latin version, followed by critical notes. It was John Colet of England who set Erasmus to producing critical editions of the New Testament.

The Strassburg reformer Martin Bucer warned his town council against multiple interpretations in a single passage of Scripture. His 1527 letter cites John Colet who in 1499 argued with Erasmus that Scripture can have but one sense, and that the simplest. Erasmus listened to Colet, describing his impact in such forcible terms that Colet "could hardly attend to anything else but the destruction of that idol of ignorance, the cobweb-divinity of the schools, and to exalt the scriptures and Jesus Christ." In his 1501 *Enchiridion* Erasmus sets forth a program of popular piety based on those Scriptures. Many vilified Erasmus. John Maier of Eck censured Erasmus from Ingolstadt on February 2, 1518. Eck carped at the new Biblical theology, "If one stagger in unbelief at the authority of sacred scripture [in Latin?] what parts will escape without suspicion of error?" Erasmus would not keep the Scripture bound in theological distinctions or in an archaic Vulgate Latin text. Long before in his *Enchiridion* Erasmus answered his critics, "To be learned falls to the lot of but few, but there is no one who cannot be a Christian, no one who cannot be pious; I may add this boldly: no one who cannot be a theologian."

The fourfold system of medieval exegesis in its literal, allegorical, anagogical, and tropological senses gave multiple insights to the Biblical scholar. In the hands of a sensitive student the text determined in its literal sense the theological expression of the church. The humanists replaced that Vulgate text with Greek editions of the New Testament and critical editions of Jerome and the Greek fathers. In replacing the Vulgate with fresh sources, the Protestant and Catholic Biblical reformers also discovered a new hermeneutic. Without that humanist return to the sources and the rejection of multiple senses in single Scriptural passages, one misses the Reformation's triumph and tragedy.

2. CHRISTOLOGICAL EXEGESIS

A reading of Luther's preface to the New Testament (1546) reflects his exegetical insights. "See to it, therefore, that you do not make a Moses out of Christ, or a book of laws and doctrines out of the gospel. . . . If I had to do without one or the other — either the work or the preaching of Christ — I would rather do without the works than without his preaching. For the works do not help me, but his words give life, as he himself says (John 6:63)."

This Christological center is the new element in Reformation interpretation. To become effective it must be preached! In its first years, word and spirit determine the exegetical contributions of the reformers. One misunderstands Luther if, like the radical Thomas Münzer, the tension is placed between letter and spirit. Luther could exercise great freedom in his use of Scripture since for him the tension was between law and gospel. The dialectic between word and spirit and gospel and law leads one directly into the great controversies between Luther and the radicals. Hans Denck summarizes the first dichotomy by attacking simple reliance on the letter of Scripture. "If a man is not in God's house, the letter is no use to him. If he is, he needs no writing to tell him God is good." Luther, as at Marburg in 1529, could hang an entire volume of divinity on a single verse of Scripture.

Ebeling describes Luther's new hermeneutics prior to 1516-1518 as unique. Luther started with the Psalms where Gordon Rupp following Vogelsang suggests his new orientation began during 1514. There the fourfold sense is rendered obsolete as the proclamation of faith in Christ appears. It was not the literalism of medieval exegesis so much as its mystical sense that silenced that proclamation. Even Aquinas who restricted exegesis to the literal sense in theological proof permitted the moral sense to dominate his hermeneutics. Lombard explained "from faith to faith" in Romans 1:17 as the movement from the "unformed faith" of James 2 to the "faith formed by charity" which is the Catholic faith "universally believed by all." Aquinas defines it, "from the faith of the Old Testament to the faith of the New Testament." Then follows a fourfold doctrinal qualification so that Aquinas loses the nature of faith in a maze of definitions. Luther's Christology is refreshing. Ebeling suggests Luther's hermeneutics was unconcerned with such verbal plays. "The fundamental problem for him is not a verbal description of God but the exposure of man's existence before God . . . the proclamation of God's judgment over man." Thus Luther exclaims in his Hebrews commentary of 1517-18: "O what a wonderful thing it is to be a Christian and to have this hidden life, not as a hermit in a cell nor in the impenetrable abysses of the human heart, but hidden in the invisible God who reveals Himself nowhere else than in the poor tokens of the Word and the hearing alone." Luther found Christ as law and gospel in both Old and New Testaments. Melanchthon taught Luther the value of Greek.

When the young Melanchthon delivered his oration on the liberal arts at Tübingen in 1517, grammar was his priority. In August, 1518 Melanchthon's inaugural address at Wittenberg so impressed Luther that he bought an edition of Homer and attended Melanchthon's class "to become a Greek." In that address he summoned his audience to drink deeply at the sources, where in the Hebrew and Greek Scriptures they would find Christ free from the discordant glosses of the Latin theologians. Luther agreed, but Eck was picqued when Melanchthon passed notes to Luther at the 1519 Leipzig debate. Luther responded, "I return to Melanchthon, whom no Eck can make me hate." Melanchthon showed Luther the Greek meaning of Hebrews 11:1-2. Luther published Melanchthon's *Lectures on Corinthians* without his permission, calling him a theologian next to Paul.

The authority of Scripture impressed Melanchthon. His *On the Church and Authority of the Word of God* expresses what Melanchthon wrote to the pastors of Saxony in April of 1550 that "The Church does not create new doctrine, but adorns the grammar of the divine words." The church cannot be bound to human succession, but only to the Word of God. Melanchthon restored the patristic exegesis of Chrysostom and Basil to the church, yet freely criticized doctrine which would not bind itself to the hermeneutical principles of faith alone and Christ alone. Where Melanchthon and Luther adorn the grammar of Scripture with faith in Christ, Zwingli insisted on the certainty and clarity of those divine words.

3. THE CLARITY OF SCRIPTURE

In his first interview with Mary, Queen of Scots, John Knox set forth the clarity of Scripture: "The word of God is plain in itself; and if there appear any obscurity in one place, the Holy Ghost, who is never contrary to Himself, explains the same more clearly in other places: so that there can remain no doubt, but to such as obstinately remain ignorant." Zwingli, too, tested everything by the light of the gospel and the fire of Paul. He remarks that philosophy and theology prevented him from devotion to the Scriptures: "But eventually came to the point where led by the Word and Spirit of God I saw the need to set aside all things and to learn the doctrine of God direct from his own Word. Then I began to ask God for light and the Scriptures became far clearer to me — even though I read nothing else — than if I had studied many commentators and expositors." Zwingli mounted the pulpit of the Great Church in Zurich, January 1, 1519 to announce a program of preaching consecutively through Matthew and ultimately the New Testament. Though Luther could not accept the militant Swiss reformer and the tragic division over the sacrament separated these leaders at Marburg in 1529, Zwingli's appeal was to divine authority.

In the Baden Disputation of 1526 Zwingli answered how one ought to listen to that Word. It must be direct and master the understanding lest one's own meaning make vain the Word of God. "If it is obscure in any place, it is to be expounded by God's Word from another place." Whether at the great disputation of January 29, 1523 or when Zwingli was at the point of death, both the preaching and hearing of the Word guided the Reformation in Zurich. There was a Zwingli Luther never knew, who wrote on October 31, 1531 before his death on the battlefield, "This is the best weapon, the only one that will be victorious, the Word of God. . . . Listen to the Word of God! That alone will set you right again." To all of this John Calvin added common sense. For the reformers Christ was the subject and sovereign of Scripture. If for Jerome to be ignorant of Scripture was to be ignorant of Christ, for them to be ignorant of Christ was to be ignorant of Scripture.

The Bible was desired in the early Reformation, says Professor Van Den Brink, as a help to find a better way to God. The Word of God "seated in the minds of the faithful" led to possession and perception of its clarity. Patrick Hamilton it seems was accused in 1528 of just that opinion that the people of Scotland were well able to understand the New Testament. In *Patrick's Places*, Hamilton expressed that better way to God:

> The Law sayeth
> Pay Thy debt
> Thou art a sinner desperate
> And Thou shalt die.
> The Gospel sayeth,
> Christ hath paid it.
> Thy sins are forgiven thee
> Be of good comfort, thou shalt be saved.

For all the reformers the clarity of Scripture led to that certainty. Its clarity and certainty provoked a crisis for Catholic exegesis.

4. CATHOLIC CRISIS

It had become fashionable to study the Bible and attend public lectures on the Scripture. All over Europe by 1540 Catholic as well as Protestant commentaries multiplied as people searched for an answer to the questions raised by the Reformation. Jedin comments that such an interest was not forced, but met a need. John Colet's Oxford lectures on St. Paul depart from medieval exegesis. When in 1496 Colet took Paul literally, Catholic exegesis entered a new age. Colet described that fascination for St. Paul in a letter. Years later he praised Erasmus' *Greek-Latin New Testament*. Parallel to Protestant Biblical study there is also a Catholic fascination for the new hermeneutic and theology. A crisis not only of vocabulary but of authority resulted.

Erasmus is well known for his influence on the followers of Valdès in Spain and the sects in Italy. Several of the reforming cardinals also wrote commentaries on St. Paul. In many of them not well known to theologians, expressions identical to those of Melanchthon occur as exegetical solutions arise from philological decisions. To select two such commentaries in the decades between Luther and Trent will clarify the crisis.

During the summer of 1535 Cardinal Sadoleto saw his *Romans Commentary* condemned in Rome. Writing under the influence of Reginald Pole in 1532, Sadoleto appealed to the Greek exegetes, especially Chrysostom and Basil. His failure is not the point; his attempt in the period of doctrinal uncertainty before Trent's 1546 decree on justification is significant. "Faith alone" occurs in several places such as his comment on Romans 1:17.

Gasparo Contarini (1483-1542) studied at Padua from 1501-1511, where he learned Greek and Patristic theology from Musurus. During Easter of 1511 the young Venetian nobleman experienced justification by faith. His letters to the Camaldolese monk, Giustiniani, describe struggles similar to those Luther endured in the monastery. By 1523 Contarini wrote that St. Paul and David are his guides; "Blessed is he to whom the Lord imputes not sin, *sine operibus.*" As a member of Pope Paul III's Reform Commission, Contarini knew the state of the

Roman church. In 1541 at Ratisbon he agreed with Eck, Bucer and Melanchthon that justification by faith was held in common by Protestant and Catholic participants. Cardinal Pole rejoiced. When Rome rejected that remarkable agreement, Contarini retired to Lucca broken in spirit. There he met the Italian, Peter Martyr Vermigli. Contarini wrote comments on the Pauline Epistles in 1542 which can not be ignored.

At Romans 1:17 Contarini writes, "From faith refers to God who promises and has given us faith. To faith truly refers to us who by assent and trust in the divine promises have received faith from God." In his Galatian notes he writes that justification is by faith in Christ. These notes written before the rigidity of Trent are the finest expression of Catholic exegesis, superior to the work of Sixtus of Siena. More careful attention to Catholic commentaries may cause a fresh reading of the Reformation, free from the study of polemic and prejudice.

Peter Martyr Vermigli shared Contarini's understanding of the nature of faith. That one died a Catholic, and the other a Protestant is incidental to an understanding of that faith. When Vermigli fled Italy, his Biblical scholarship was welcomed on the continent and in England. For Vermigli the clarity of Scripture is essential. His views summarize the crisis provoked by the new Reformation hermeneutic. In his *Common Places* Vermigli argues, "But yet this perspicuity is not to be sought at the light of man's sense and reason; but at the light of faith, whereby we ought to be most certainlie persuaded of whatsoever is contained in the holie Scriptures." The dream of Protestant and Catholic Biblical theologians for unity turned to a nightmare in the reactionary theology of Trent. And ever since, both parties have argued whether Scripture authorizes bishops or bishops authorize Scripture. *The Scots Confession of 1560* formulates one answer to that crisis of authority: "As we believe and confess the Scriptures of God sufficient to instruct and make the man of God perfect, so do we affirm and avow the authority of the same to be of God, and neither to depend on men nor angels. We affirm therefore that such as allege the Scripture to have no [other] authority, but that which is received from the Kirk, to be blasphemous against God and injurious to the true Kirk, which always heareth and obeyeth the voice of her own Spouse and Pastor, but taketh not upon her to be mistress over the same."

BIBLIOGRAPHY

Bainton, Roland, "The Bible In The Reformation," *The Cambridge History of The Bible, The West From the Reformation To The Present Day*. Cambridge University Press, 1963, 1-37.

Davies, Rupert E., *The Problem of Authority in the Continental Reformers*. London: The Epworth Press, 1946.

Duhamel, P. Albert, "The Oxford Lectures of John Colet," *Journal of the History of Ideas*," XIV (1953), 493-510.

Ebeling, Gerhard, "The New Hermeneutics and

The Early Luther," *Theology Today,* XXI (1964-65), 34-46.

Grimm, Harold J., "Lorenzo Valla's Christianity," *Church History,* XVIII (1949), 75-88.

Harbison, E. Harris, *The Christian Scholar in the Age of The Reformation.* New York: Charles Scribner's Sons, 1956.

Kooiman, Willem Jan, *Luther and the Bible.* Philadelphia: Muhlenberg Press, 1961.

Lehman, Paul L., "The Reformers' Use of the Bible," *Theology Today,* III (1946), 328-344.

Mann Phillips, Margaret, *Erasmus and the Northern Renaissance.* London: English Universities Press, 1949.

Manschreck, Clyde, *Melanchthon On Christian Doctrine.* New York: Oxford University Press, 1965, vii-xlii.

McNeill, John T., "The Significance of the Word of God for Calvin," *Church History* 28 (1959), 131-146.

Montgomery, John Warwick, "Sixtus of Siena and Roman Catholic Biblical Scholarship in the Reformation Period," *Archiv für Reformationsgeschichte* 54 (1963), 214-233.

Prenter, Regin, "The Living Word," *More About Luther.* Decorah, Iowa: Luther College Press, 1958, 65-80.

Rupp, E. Gordon, "The Bible in the Age of the Reformation," D. E. Nineham, *The Church's Use of the Bible Past and Present.* London: S.P.C.K., 1963, 73-87.

Rupp, E. Gordon, "Word and Spirit in the First Years of the Reformation," *Archiv für Reformationsgeschichte* 49 (1958), 13-25.

Van Den Brink, J. N. Bakhuizen, "Bible and Biblical Theology in the Early Reformation," *Scottish Journal of Theology* 14 (1961), 337-352; 15 (1962), 50-65.

Wallace, Ronald S., *Calvin's doctrine of the Word and Sacrament*. Edinburgh: Oliver and Boyd, 1953.

Zwingli, Huldrych, "Of the Clarity and Certainty of the Word of God," *Library of Christian Classics*, Vol. XXIV. Philadelphia: The Westminster Press, MCMLIII, 49-95.

7

Interpretation of Prophecy

The interpretation of Biblical prophecy is a specific kind of Biblical interpretation. Valid principles of Biblical hermeneutics should therefore apply. However, this is not always admitted, and, as Ramm points out, "the real issue in prophetic interpretation among evangelicals is this: *can prophetic literature be interpreted by the general method of grammatical exegesis, or is some special principle necessary?* (*Protestant Biblical Interpretation*, 2d ed., p. 225). In this article we shall defend the position that prophecy is to be interpreted according to the same principles that apply in all Biblical study.

1. PROPHECY AND THE PROPHETS

To attempt to discuss prophecy without a thorough understanding of the prophetic movement in Israel is to open the door to every sort of subjectivity. The various kinds of interpretation applied to prophecy range from orthodoxy to the "lunatic fringe," and include denominational and sectarian groups, cultic and schismatic movements, and heretical and fanatical extremists. Merely to look at the list of groups or movements that base their right to existence upon Biblical prophecy would convince any reasonable Biblical scholar that an objective basis for the study of prophecy is of primary importance. The study of the Biblical prophetic movement provides such an objective basis.

Discussions of the terms "prophet" and "seer" can be found in Bible dictionaries and Biblical theologies. Here we can only point out that the prophets were historic persons who spoke to their contemporaries out of historical situations. The basic meaning of prophet is "to speak forth," and foretelling is but one aspect of forthtelling. A large part of the prophetic writings in the Bible deals not with prediction of things to come but with God's judgment on the behavior of his people. It is a mistake, however, to deny or ignore the predictive element of prophecy, for in declaring the judgment of God the prophet sets forth what God is threatening to do and what the outcome of God's judgment will be. Some idea of the meaning of prophet may be gained from the fact that in the Hebrew canon, the books of Joshua, Judges, Samuel, and Kings are called "the Former Prophets," and these books are almost devoid of predictive prophecy.

2. MESSIANIC PROPHECY

The interpretation of messianic prophecy should follow the same rules that apply for all prophecy. If this is done, we soon discover that some of the prophecies we have considered "messianic" either are not such or are messianic only in the fuller meaning. The word Messiah (literally "anointed"), as applied to the messianic king of David's line, does not occur at all in the Old Testament, with the possible exception of Daniel 9:25-26. There are, however, many prophecies of the Davidic king to come and of the age he is to establish. The number of such prophecies and the details contained in them increase as we move toward the time of the advent of Christ. The word Christ ("anointed") comes from the Greek translation of the Hebrew word for Messiah. We would do well to remind ourselves that most of those who lived in the time of the coming of Christ so misinterpreted prophecy that they failed to recognize the Messiah.

3. APOCALYPTIC PROPHECY

A special type of messianic prophecy is apocalyptic (such as Daniel and Revelation), in which the message is set forth almost entirely in symbolic language. Even here, the only sure guide is to begin with the literal interpretation, using "literal" in the sense to be defined. For the interpretation of the symbols "literally," we need to know the historical significance of those symbols at the time and the place of the writing. There is almost certainly no universal symbolism, as Davidson points out, but there is a regularity in the symbolism used by any given author, and sometimes this carries over from one work to another (as, e.g., in the case of the use of Daniel in Revelation). A warning should be expressed concerning the symbolism of numbers, colors, and materials, but at the same time it must be admitted that there is a high degree of regularity in the symbolic use of certain numbers (such as 7, 12, 40), and perhaps a lesser degree in the symbolic use of colors (such as white, red, and black).

4. REJECTED METHODS OF INTERPRETATION

Although confusion in terminology complicates the problem, modern scholars are basically in agreement that the allegorical method, according to which the true meaning is not in the words but in the allegorizing of the words; the mystical method, which looks for the meaning in such things as the numerical values of letters; and the dogmatic method, which reduces the Bible to a collection of proof-texts, along with modern developments of these methods, are all unsatisfactory. For a full discussion, see F. W. Farrar, *History of Interpretation,* and for a summary, B. Ramm, *op. cit.,* Chap. II.

An illustration of the allegorical method is Origen's treatment of Genesis 24:16, "[Rebecca was] a virgin, neither had any man known her"; which means, says Origen, that Christ is the husband of the soul when it is converted, and that Satan becomes the husband of the soul when it falls away (see Farrar, *op. cit.,* p. 199). The mystical method can be demonstrated by the rabbinical exegesis of the words "until Shiloh come" (Gen. 49:10). Since the numerical value of the letters in the words Shiloh shall come is 358, which is also the numerical value of the word Messiah, Shiloh means the Messiah. Examples of the proof-text method can be found almost everywhere, but many of them are accepted because the text is used to support a true theological tenet. When we turn to sectarian movements, such as Jehovah's Witnesses or Christian Science, we soon become aware of the weakness of the method. But one example of questionable proof-text methodology is to be found in the orthodox evangelical's use of the "jot or tittle" passage (Matt. 5:18) to "prove" the doctrine of verbal inspiration. Jesus was talking about the teachings of the Scripture, not about jots and tittles nor about words; some of these teachings were already fulfilled and were passing away as Jesus spoke (e.g., Moses' teaching on divorce, Matt. 5:32; 19:3-8), and many more would be swept away by the Epistle to the Hebrews. Yet it remains true that the law and the prophets were not destroyed; they were fulfilled. The verbal inspiration of the Scriptures was not questioned by his hearers, nor was it defended by Jesus: it was accepted by them.

5. THE LITERAL INTERPRETATION

The basic meaning of any Biblical prophecy is that which the author intended his hearers or readers to understand. Since we begin with the faith that God communicated with prophets, we must therefore recognize that we are speaking not only (a) of what the prophet intended his hearers to understand, but also (b) of what God intended the prophet to understand in each instance. However, let us hold this latter part of the discussion until we have clarified the former.

As many authors have noted the very

word "literal" introduces a few problems. For example, when a writer or speaker makes use of common figures of speech, a "literal" interpretation accepts the figures of speech as figures. In every kind of communication (except the Bible, according to some interpreters), the common figures of speech are readily recognized and interpreted as such. This principle must be applied also in Biblical study. "The moon (shall be turned) into blood" (Joel 2:31), interpreted literally, means that the moon's color shall become blood-red, and not that the moon actually becomes blood. When God tells Jeremiah, "I am calling all the tribes of the kingdoms of the north" (Jer. 1:15 RSV), he is using hyperbole; it is not necessary to interpret "all" to mean every tribe without exception. Nor does the Lord intend the words in Jeremiah 1:18 to mean that Jeremiah is actually to become "a fortified city, an iron pillar, and bronze walls" (RSV). "Literal" interpretation means the understanding which any person of normal intelligence would get, without any special spiritual gifts and without any "code" or "key."

The literal interpretation of a prophecy is the only basis of objectivity. Without it, any interpreter, with his own system, can make any prophecy mean anything — and history has certainly shown that men and women will do just that. Every sect and schismatic group calling itself Biblical is able to find Biblical support for its doctrines. It is the hermeneutics used, the method of Biblical interpretation which they apply, that makes such confusing and contradictory claims possible. Only when we start with the literal interpretation can we establish objective guidelines for the testing of other interpretations.

So important is this principle that A. B. Davidson says,

"This I consider the first principle in prophetic interpretation — to read the prophet literally — to assume that the literal meaning is *his* meaning — that he is moving among realities, not symbols, among concrete things like peoples, not among abstractions like *our* Church, world, etc. If we make this assumption, then we know what we have before us" (*Old Testament Prophecy,* pp. 167-168).

He insists that "there is no pervasive symbolism in the prophetic language" (p. 160); in other words, we are not to give such terms as "mountain," "horn," "star," "sea," etc., regular symbolic meanings and then read these meanings back into prophecies wherever the terms occur. There is symbolism, of course, for the prophets, who received many of their revelations in the form of visions, were obliged to express many truths in symbolic form. We shall return to this later. But, says Davidson, this symbolism can be understood by us without a "system" just as it was understandable to the prophet's hearers. "The first thing in interpreting prophecy is to hold that the prophet had a meaning, that he uses language like any other writer, and that what he literally says he literally means. Thus, and thus alone, can we reach his meaning" (p. 168).

6. SYMBOLS AND TYPES

To speak of "symbolic" meaning does not necessarily imply a departure from the literal meaning. We can speak "literally" of certain facts, of persons and places and things, of actions, of concrete realities. But when we begin to speak of ideas and concepts, we find that we must often resort to the use of figures of speech in order to convey meaning. And the less the concept is related to the experience of the reader, the more important the use of symbol becomes.

Every formula or equation in mathematics, chemistry, physics, symbolic logic, and many other subjects, is written in symbols and is interpreted literally. The face of the clock, the keyboard of the typewriter, and the page of a musical score are covered with symbols. Certain symbols are capable of two or more meanings. The symbol "3" — which generally conveys the abstract idea of threeness — may indicate the route a bus can be expected to take, or the name of a football player. In combination, such as 3/4/66, it may suggest the month of March or (to a European) the third day of April, whereas 3/4 — might be read as three pounds four shillings, and 3'4" could be read as three feet four inches. To a Frenchman or a German, it would be pronounced entirely different. And the amazing fact is that most of us never stop and ask, "How is it possible to know which interpretation is the right one?" The human mind is able to set the symbol against its context and interpret it, in most cases, instantly.

When we speak about God, who is spirit and not flesh, who inhabits eternity, who is completely "other" except for whatever portion of his image may be found in us, symbolic language is almost the only means we have to describe him. When we call Him "Father" we are taking a reality from our world-system, and using it to convey certain truth about God. When we say that God "hears" us, we likewise are using symbol, for hearing is a phenomenon which requires first the production of sound waves in the atmosphere, then some physical means of receiving these sound waves and converting them to sensory stimuli in our human nervous system, and finally the connecting of these stimuli with the corresponding "bits" that have been stored in our brain as "memory," so that the present stimuli and past experiences are properly paired and the hearer receives the message which the speaker was attempting to communicate. Obviously, when we say that God "hears" we are not implying that he has the physical organs necessary for hearing, or that he is dependent on our atmosphere for the transmission of the sound waves. As a matter of fact, we believe that we can pray silently and he can still "hear" us.

In the Bible certain revelations of truth are presented through symbols which at a future time are to be replaced by reality. Such a symbol is properly called a type.

An excellent illustration of a type is the tabernacle, which was a symbol of the presence of the Lord (Yahweh). The tabernacle was called *mishkan*, "dwelling place," and *ohel*, "tent," words which clearly indicate the symbolism. The significance is further defined by the presence of the pillar of cloud over the tabernacle and by the statement that "everyone who sought the Lord would go out to the tent of meeting" (Exod. 33:7 RSV). We are not to understand, of course, that the Lord actually was confined in the tabernacle or that his presence was only to be found between the cherubim of the mercy seat, for he inhabits eternity, as Solomon correctly recognized (II Chron. 6:18). But in a special way the Lord was present in the midst of his people Israel, and the tabernacle was a symbol of that fact. Later, the tabernacle was replaced by the temple, and the temple became the symbol of the Lord's presence. But the presence of the Lord became a reality in the incarnation, and the symbol became unnecessary, hence it is proper to speak of the tabernacle as a *type* of the incarnate Son of God. As a matter of fact, the New Testament suggests this very idea in the words, "And the Word became flesh and dwelt (tabernacled) among us" (John 1:14).

It is possible to develop this idea even further, and to say that the tabernacle (or temple) is also a type of the presence of the Spirit of God in the body of the believer, for our body is called the "temple of the Holy Spirit" (I Cor. 6:19) and "the temple of the living God" (II Cor. 6:16).

The full and final fulfillment, of course, is found in the Holy City, the New Jerusalem, of which John said, "I saw no temple in the city, for its temple is the Lord God the Almighty and the Lamb" (Rev. 21:22 RSV). In this respect, the presence of God in the Holy City can be looked upon as the antitype of the tabernacle and the temple.

A number of writers hold that any person, place, thing, or action in Scripture can be a type. In my opinion, this is an extension of the meaning of type which is both unwarranted and dangerous. Joseph, for example, is sometimes called "a type of Christ." But Joseph is Joseph, a real or historical person, whose existence shall continue into the age to come. He is not a symbol that shall one day be replaced by a reality; he is a reality. It would be more proper to say that certain facets of his life are symbolic, such as the rejection by his brothers, his exaltation to a place of authority, his forgiveness of his brothers, etc. Perhaps these symbols could be called "types" of Christ's similar experiences, but even this usage is open to abuse. According to some teachers, if a whole is typical, then the parts are also typical. On this basis, the details of the tabernacle and its furnishings are considered as types, and a significance is sought in each detail, with an antitype in Christ. Strictly speaking, this is an application of the allegorical method, rather than the typical.

The extremes to which some interpreters have gone in finding types in Scripture have led many scholars in recent decades to reject the entire notion. More recently, however, the subject has been recognized as valid, and discussions of typology can be found in several works. For example, G. von Rad says,

". . . we do introduce a new element of interpretation which does not derive from the Old Testament in that we presuppose the existence of a particular kind of connexion between the saving events of the Old Testament and the transcendent saving events of the New. . . . The name given to such exegesis is relatively unimportant. If it is called typological, the term is a suitable one. . . . And yet the essence of our view differs from earlier typology . . .; we, however, can no longer say that the David or Joshua of history, or the Tabernacle, or the Passover lamb, are types of Christ [*Old Testament Theology*, Vol. II, p. 371.]

It is in this sense — i.e., in the light of a final fulfilment and of the ceaseless movement towards such a fulfilment — that we can speak of a prophetic power resident in the Old Testament prototypes." (*Ibid.*, p. 373.)

The present discussion does not follow von Rad except in the basic principle. But that principle is important. The basis for typology must be found in the organismic redemptive and the progressive revelatory activity of God. This principle underlies the argument presented by the Epistle to the Hebrews. Since the fall of Adam, there has been only one way of salvation, namely, by the gracious redeeming activity of God. But there has been a divine educational process or revelation unfolding through the ages until the final redemptive act in his Son. Otherwise, why was Christ not crucified by Cain? We are forced to assume that the education of the race, particularly of God's representative people, was a necessary part of God's plan. But if the entire redemptive process was organismic, i.e., if each step was intended to present the basic truth that redemption was provided by God and received by faith, then we may rightly conclude that the use of symbols and types necessarily had to precede the actual event. Accordingly, von Rad correctly states that, "No special hermeneutic method is necessary to see the whole diversified movement of the Old Testament saving events, made up of God's promises and their temporary fulfilments, as pointing to their future fulfilment in Jesus Christ. This can be said quite categorically. The coming of Jesus Christ as a historical reality leaves the exegete no choice at all; he must interpret the Old Testament as pointing to Christ, whom he must understand in its light" (*ibid.*, p. 374).

7. THE FULLER OR DEEPER MEANING

Roman Catholic scholars in recent Biblical studies often speak of the *sensus plenior*, or "fuller meaning," a term attributed to Andrea Fernández in an article written in 1925. Raymond E. Brown in his dissertation on the subject offers the following definition: "The *sensus plenior* is that additional, deeper meaning, intended by God but not clearly intended by the human author, which is seen to exist in the words of a Biblical text (or group

106

of texts, or even a whole book) when they are studied in the light of further revelation or development in the understanding of revelation" (*The Sensus Plenior of Sacred Scripture*, p. 92).

Protestant scholars have sometimes indicated a similar idea, but discussions of the subject are confused because of the terminology used. The terms spiritual, mystical, allegorical, and typological, as Ramm has shown (*Protestant Biblical Interpretation*, 2d ed., p. 223), are variously used and often overlap. We suggest that the adoption of the term *sensus plenior* or its English translation will help to clarify the problem. In his study, Brown differentiates between the "literal" sense and the "fuller" sense on the basis of the human author's clear intention. If the divine author intended more in the revelation than the human author intended to convey to his hearers or readers, this is the fuller meaning (or *sensus plenior*) of the passage. Some will object, insisting that the human author was never derogated to a position where he became a mere scribe who wrote without understanding. I would agree in principle with such an objection, for inspiration, as I understand it, is the action of the Spirit upon the author by which the author becomes the recipient of God's revelation. This action does not reduce or destroy the personal knowledge or ability of the human author, nor does it superimpose a knowledge or ability which he does not normally have; but rather it heightens, or deepens, or makes more sensitive his natural ability so that he sees what God wants him to see, hears what God wants him to hear, and communicates this under the influence of the same Spirit.

But is it not possible for God to present to the author a revelation which by its very nature contains a deeper significance? Perhaps the author, under inspiration, could see the deeper meaning, perhaps not — this is incidental to any given revelation. In either event, the author does not intentionally convey the *sensus plenior* to his hearers. But at a later date, in the light of further revelation, the fuller meaning becomes clear to readers under the influence of the Spirit who inspired the original author. At a lower level, it is true that great poets, philosophers, and other creative thinkers often express a fuller meaning — perhaps even without knowing it — which their "disciples" develop into schools or systems of thought. If a human author can send forth a message which has a *sensus plenior*, why is it unthinkable that a divinely inspired author could do the same?

Brown further distinguishes the *sensus plenior* from the "typical" sense by relating the fuller sense to the words and the typical sense to the things or actions set forth by the words. He admits that there are borderline cases where the *sensus plenior* and the typical sense can scarcely be distinguished.

8. APPLICATIONS OF THESE PRINCIPLES

At this point it may be helpful to use a few Scriptural passages to clarify the discussion. In Genesis 3:15 there is the *Protevan-*

gelium (or first form of the gospel), sometimes taken to be a prophecy of the Messiah
and even of the virgin birth: "I will put
enmity between you and the woman, and
between your seed and her seed; he shall
bruise your head, and you shall bruise his
heel" (RSV). The literal sense of the passage is clear. God is speaking to the serpent
who has led Eve into the sin of disobeying
God's revelation. God is saying that there
will be hostility between human beings (the
seed of the woman) and serpents (the seed
of the serpent), in the course of which human beings will be hurt (bruising of the
heel) and serpents will be killed (bruising
of the head). But certainly this is hardly
worthy of the setting of the story. There
must be a deeper meaning. The *sensus
plenior* might be expressed as follows: The
spiritual crisis (temptation and fall) was
brought about by a being (the serpent) hostile to God and his revealed will. This hostility will continue to be expressed throughout
the ages, and human beings will be hurt by
it. But at last there will be victory, because a
certain man (whom we identify with Jesus
Christ from later revelation) will finally destroy the tempter (whom we identify with
Satan from later revelation). Is there also a
typical meaning? Can we say that Eve is a
type of Mary? Possibly in her name (Gen.
3:20) and in her statement when Cain
was born (Gen. 4:1) she is a type of Mary
— but I am inclined to reject such typology.
Can we say that the "seed" of the woman is
a type of Christ? I think not, for the seed of
the woman is the human race, and in the

fuller sense it is Christ. But a type, we have seen, is a symbol that is later replaced by a reality, and certainly the human race was not replaced by Christ.

In Ezekiel 34, God pronounces judgment upon false shepherds, and declares that he will search for his sheep, concluding with the words, "I will set up over them one shepherd, my servant David, and he shall feed them: he shall feed them and be their shepherd" (34:23 RSV). Is David a type of Christ? In this case, the language is perfectly clear, and there is little reason to seek a *sensus plenior*. But from the Christian viewpoint, it is Jesus and not David who is both shepherd and prince (cf. 34:34). Yet we know that David is not a symbol, later to be replaced by Jesus; David is a person with immortality. It would be more correct, in my opinion, to speak of the Davidic office or the throne of David as the type.

Even more accurately we can speak of the son of David as the type. This is particularly noteworthy in the promise made to David, when he desired to build a house for the Lord, and the Lord said, "When your days are fulfilled and you lie down with your fathers, I will raise up your son after you, who shall come forth from your body, and I will establish his kingdom. He shall build a house for my name, and I will establish the throne of his kingdom for ever" (II Sam. 7:12-13 RSV). It is clear from verses 14-15 that God is speaking of the actual son of David, whom we know to be Solomon, for God speaks of the iniquity that he will commit. Moreover, we know that

Solomon did build the temple. On the other hand, we also know that Solomon's kingdom ended in civil war and the secession of the northern tribes. Furthermore, it is always the throne of David, and not the throne of Solomon, that is mentioned in prophecy (cf. Isa. 9:7; Luke 1:32). And again, it is recorded that David referred to this son as "Lord" (Ps. 110:1; cf. Matt. 22:43-45). Since the throne of David becomes the throne of the Messiah, we may speak of David's throne as a type, and since Solomon is replaced ultimately by the Messiah on that throne, it is possible to speak either of the fuller meaning of the expression "David's son," or to say that Solomon, in this office, is a type of Christ.

How shall we understand the prophecies in Isaiah chapters 7-11? Literally, Isaiah 7 deals with King Ahaz of Judah and the Syro-Ephraimite coalition of Rezin of Syria and Pekah of Israel (7:1), including a sign which the Lord was giving to indicate that Ahaz had nothing to fear from them (7:7-9). The sign was to be in the birth of a child called "Immanuel" (7:14), and the sudden solution of the Syro-Ephraimite problem in the face of a greater problem, namely the king of Assyria (7:17). The fuller meaning is to be found in the fact that Israel's basic problem was not the unbelief of Ahaz, but that of the people, and the ultimate solution was not in the temporary removal of national foes but in the permanent removal of all unbelief. Hence the Christian church, following Matthew 1:23, has seen the birth of Jesus Christ to be the fulfillment of the prophecy. The virgin birth of Jesus, we should note, in no way depends on Isaiah 7:14, but on the unequivocal statements in Matthew (1:18, 25) and Luke (1:34, 35).

Isaiah 9 is of a different nature. Here Isaiah is clearly talking about a coming ruler (9:6), whose reign fits the description of the messianic reign given elsewhere (Jer. 23:5; cf. II Sam. 7:12-16). Whether Isaiah was privileged to understand the details of his prophecy we cannot tell. Quite likely this is a case of "prophetic foreshortening" or "prophetic perspective," terms often used to describe the phenomenon in which the prophet sees the near-at-hand and the distant in the same plane. Following the prophecy concerning Rezin and Pekah and concerning the king of Assyria (8:6-7), Isaiah sees light breaking through the darkness (8:22; 9:1). To judge by the words that follow (10:5-11, 20-27, especially v. 25), it would seem that Isaiah expected this light to dawn "in a very little while." We know, from New Testament revelation, that Isaiah was seeing the return from exile, the first advent of Christ, and the millennial kingdom at one time, without any indication of intervals between them.

Isaiah 11 offers an illustration of symbolic language, as well as prophetic foreshortening. The "shoot from the stump of Jesse" and its parallel "branch out of his roots" is obviously symbolic language referring to the remnant of Israel (see 6:13). The prophecy could, therefore, pertain to the remnant after the exile, and "him" in 11:2 could mean the remnant of the nation. However, verses 3 and 4 pick up some of the language of the messianic king (cf. Ps. 2:8-9; 72:12-14), and verses 6-9 present the idyllic age of the Messiah. We must therefore look for the fuller meaning, which, we know from New Testament revelation, includes both advents of Christ.

The "Royal Psalms" offer another area of study which is instructive. Since several passages from these Psalms have been quoted in the Epistle to the Hebrews, it is very difficult for the Christian to come to the original passages without a Christian interpretation already built in. But certainly, the men and women who heard and used these Psalms had no such knowledge of Christ; if they had had such a clear understanding, they would never have rejected Jesus and his claims. The "Royal Psalms" — ignoring in this article the entire problem of the New Year's festival, the enthronement ritual, and related matters — were clearly addressed to or sung in honor of the reigning king of Israel (see Ps. 45:1). But we must remember that the king who occupied the throne of David was heir to the promise made to David. He was David's "son" and his throne was David's throne. As such, it was an eternal throne, and divine titles could be ascribed to it and, in a sense, to its occupant. For example, the occupant could be called God's "son" (Ps. 2:7). It is possible that the king as God's vicegerent could be addressed as "God" — for it is an open question whether Psalm 45:6 should be translated "thy throne, O God, is for ever and ever" or "thy throne is God for ever and ever" (in the Greek of Hebrews 1:8 the same possibility occurs). Even Psalm 110 was doubtless addressed to the king, and was an assurance of the Lord's fidelity to his promise. But, as we have seen, the Davidic throne is a type of the Messianic throne, and we know from New Testament revelation that the Messiah is not merely a human king of David's line but is the incarnate Son of God. The *sensus plenior*, therefore, of Psalm 110 concerns the greater Son of David, who is in fact David's Lord.

Within the limits of this article it is impossible to take up every prophecy, or even a representative of each kind of prophecy. The mention of Bethlehem in Micah 5:2 can be taken in the literal sense merely as an indication that the line of David had not been rejected, for Micah was obviously thinking of his own day (see 5:5). But the fuller meaning refers to the messianic king, hence the Christian sees the fulfillment in the birth of Jesus.

The "servant of the Lord" in Isaiah 42-53 is somewhat more complex. Israel was the servant of the Lord (Isa. 41:8; 44:1), but Israel was an unfaithful servant and suffered because of disobedience. The remnant of Israel was the Lord's servant of whom it could be said that the righteous suffer for the sins of the unrighteous. Some of the expressions in Isaiah 53 could properly be applied to the remnant. The more obedient the servant of the Lord, the more he will be despised and rejected of men. Accordingly, the fuller meaning of the servant passages has to do with the perfect Servant, and the Christian rightly identifies this Servant with the one who came in the form of a servant and who was obedient even unto death (cf. Phil. 2:7-8).

For an illustration of apocalyptic prophecy we may turn to Daniel 7. Since this is a dream or vision in highly symbolic form (7:1), the literal interpretation requires an attempt to understand the author's meaning intended by the symbols. This is often difficult or even impossible in apocalyptic literature, but in Daniel 7 we have the author's interpretation. The "beasts" are kingdoms (7:12, 23) or their rulers (7:17), and the "horns" are kings (7:7, 24). They are obviously hostile to God's rule and persecute his people, and this hostility comes to a climax in the time of the fourth kingdom, especially under the terrible king who comes to the throne after ten who preceded him (7:21, 25). However, he does not have the final word, for "one that was ancient of days" (7:9) is in control, and the rule, an everlasting dominion (7:14), is given to "one like a son of man" (7:13), while the kingdoms of the world are delivered for ever to the "saints of the Most High" (7:27). Clearly, the author is foretelling the triumph of God's king over the kings of the world. To attempt to identify the individual kingdoms and kings is difficult, for it requires not only a thorough knowledge of the history of the period but also a knowledge of the symbolism and common expressions of the day. We can, however, carry over the symbolic interpretation to other parts of Daniel's prophecy, so that we can understand the heart of his message. When it comes to setting dates or charting the future, it is just at those points where we usually become dogmatic that we should become most humble. It is an infallible rule of prophetic interpretation that the prophecy becomes fully clear only after it has been fulfilled.

Using these principles of interpretation, we are objective and reasonable. There is nothing cultic or fantastic in the interpretations. The literal meaning is always definitive, and both the fuller meaning and the typical interpretation are developed from the literal. Scripture is compared with Scripture, but never in such way as to distort the historical or grammatical sense of the passages used in the comparison. The "theological" interpretation is not imposed on Scripture as in proof-text methodology, but rather the Bible becomes the source of theology. If this method demands more of our time and effort than other methods, this is as it should be, for in this as in all matters we usually get what we pay for. Above all, both the inspiration of the Spirit in the original revelation and inscripturation, and the illumination of the Spirit in the interpretation are duly honored. It is God's Word, and we must let God tell us what it means.

BIBLIOGRAPHY

Beecher, W. J., *The Prophets and the Promise,* 1905, reprint 1963.

Berkhof, L., *Principles of Biblical Interpretation,* 2nd ed., 1952.

Brown, R. E., *The Sensus Plenior of Sacred Scripture,* 1955.

Davidson, A. B., *Old Testament Prophecy,* 1904.

Farrar, F. W., *History of Interpretation*, 1886. reprint 1961.

Kevan, E. F., "The Principles of Interpretation," *Revelation and the Bible* (C. F. H. Henry, ed.), 1958.

Oehler, G. F., *Theology of the Old Testament*, Part II, Prophetism, 1883.

Ramm, Bernard, *Protestant Biblical Interpretation*, rev. ed., 1956.

Synave, P. and Benoit, P., *Prophecy and Inspiration*, Eng. tr., 1961.

von Hofmann, J. C. K., *Interpreting the Bible*, Eng. tr., 1959.

von Rad, G., *Old Testament Theology*, Vol. II, Eng. tr., 1965.

8

Typological Interpretation of the Old Testament

The history of the Christian church has shown clearly that the advent of Christ and the New Testament has raised problems in the minds of many regarding the relevance of the Old Testament. At one extreme was Marcion (A.D. 85) who sought to expunge any reference to a fierce God from the Bible, and so rejected the Old Testament *in toto,* as well as much of the New Testament. At the other extreme were the church fathers (with their followers today) who sought to retain the Old Testament by fanciful allegorical and typological interpretation. In allegory, history is of little importance, and thus the literal meaning of a text is overlooked. The persons and things and events in a document supposedly stand for spiritual processes and actions and essences, for timeless truths already predetermined from other sources. In typology, however, history and literal meaning are taken seriously. Here a person or thing or event, which had a real existence and significance of its own, symbolizes or represents or prefigures someone or something greater at a later time. But, in either case, the reason for the approach is the question regarding the relevance of the old covenant. In recent days there has come a revival of interest in typology among Biblical scholars in a renewed attempt to answer this. It is not a return to the extreme typological approach of the Fathers, who saw a correspondence between Old and New Testament in minute details, but rather a stress on a general correspondence between the events and figures and institutions of both Testaments.

1. THE OLD TESTAMENT EVIDENCE

In the life and worship of Israel there was a constant re-interpretation and re-presentation of the original revelatory acts of God, because God's will and actions were seen as basically the same in any age. Thus Israel did not distinguish very clearly between the past and the present. At the great annual festivals of pilgrimage, during which time all adult male Israelites had to appear at the sanctuaries, the important events of Israel's history were "re-presented." The feast of passover and unleavened bread was celebrated year by year in the month the Lord delivered Israel from Egypt (Deut. 16:1). Its purpose was to "remember" the events of the Exodus experience, and unleavened bread was eaten to recreate the original time of haste. This meant that annually Israel was reliving the situation of being prepared for setting-out, for deliverance from bondage. The same was true with the feast of tabernacles or booths (Lev. 23:43). The means of "re-presentation" was primarily by a retelling of the story of what God did for his people (Exod. 12:24ff.), although cultic drama may also have entered in (cf. Ps. 24). We also see this in the book of Deuteronomy, where the *parenetic* discourses are characterized by the frequently occurring expression "today," the purpose of which was to make the contemporary listener hear the law as if it were for the first time and as if it were directed solely at him, as if he were at Mt. Sinai (cf. Deut. 5:3; 6:21; 26:16-19). The important point to realize is that these "representations" were made, not merely to glory in the past (as if it were an ancient Fourth of July celebration), but that the present Israel might continually be taught the nature of the God she served and the response that was necessary, for God was active in the same way in the present. The wilderness wandering, for example, was retold to show the result of rebelliousness among the fathers, but also to warn the present people of a similar fate if they also rebelled.

But, furthermore, Israel also looked to the future, and saw a correspondence between it and the past. G. von Rad has pointed out in *Essays on Old Testament Hermeneutics* (pp. 17-39), that the Old Testament form of "analogy" or "typology" is quite different from that found in non-Israelite thought. Outside of Israel one finds a mythological conception of an all-embracing correspondence between heavenly and earthly things. All countries, rivers, cities, temples, etc. on earth were conceived to be only copies of the prototypes which existed in heaven. But in Israelite thought, on the contrary, there was an historical analogy between eschatological events and beginning events. Thus Amos and Isaiah speak of the eschatological return of the Paradise experience (Amos 9:13; Isa. 11:6-8). Amos also looks for the return of David (Amos 9:11), and Hosea and Isaiah mention the return of the wilderness days (Hos. 2:14-20; Isa. 52; 11-12). These prophets were not simply predicting that a particular historical event would recur. They saw a pattern in God's actions, or the repetition of a similar kind of event. It would not be merely another David; a greater than David would come. It would not be an exact return of a wilderness experience, but a greater deliverance from bondage.

This means, on the one hand, that the Old Testament writers saw a continuity to history. The judgments and acts of redemption in the Old Testament were a prefiguration of the Christ event in the New. As von Rad writes, "the same God who revealed himself in Christ has also left his footprints in the history of the Old Testament covenant people . . . we have to do with one divine discourse, here to the fathers through the prophets, there to us through Christ (Heb. 1:1)" (*op cit.*, p. 36). But it also means on the other hand, that from the standpoint of the New Testament we see meanings in the Old that the original authors missed, because the coming of Christ illumines the action of God in Israel. However, one must be careful to make a distinction between typology (or, correspondence, analogy) and allegory. One cannot

121

look for correspondence in details or find hidden spiritual meanings, but rather must seek historical analogies alone.

W. Zimmerli in *Essays on Old Testament Hermeneutics* (pp. 89-122), has clarified this typological interpretation by his scheme of "promise and fulfillment." He distinguishes carefully between "prediction" and "promise." Prediction is the illumination of future events, but promise is the understanding that God has determined to accomplish his purposes, and is already working towards the completion of this goal. It is not just a word about something that is to come; it speaks of a future already in progress of fulfillment. Zimmerli stresses that the Old Testament depicts God's actions in history as a series of promises (not predictions) and fulfillments, with each fulfillment giving rise to the expectation of a greater fulfillment in the future. This is because the promises of God were never exhausted by one fulfillment. So the promise of rest in the promised land (Deut 12:9; 25:19) was apparently fulfilled in the conquest under Joshua (Josh. 21:45), but this was not meant to imply a final fulfillment, as Joshua 23:15-16 indicates when it looks to the possibility of the destruction of that rest, and as Hebrews 4:1ff. clarifies when it shows that Canaan was not the final intended rest. And this same movement can be seen throughout the Old Testament. In the latter prophets the final fulfillment of promise becomes eschatological, showing that the fulfillments in Israel were only the beginning phase of God's plan.

The prophets found a typological significance in the historical events which enabled them to speak relevantly about God's next acts in history. So when Christ came and "actualized" the promises, he ensured the validity of the Old Testament by showing that it is part of the same divine program. Thus the Old Testament is valuable for the church, because here we can see our own situation before God, since we are still on the road to the final enrichment of that fulfillment, and so can live in trust that God fulfills his promises.

2. THE NEW TESTAMENT EVIDENCE

The coming of Christ is represented in the New Testament as something both totally new, and yet as having roots and foregleams in the Old Testament. This is centered in the *kerygma* or "proclamation of the gospel." In its fundamental form the *kerygma* consists of the proclamation of certain historical events in a context which interprets the significance of those events. The events are basically (1) the life, death, and resurrection of Jesus, and (2) the development of the church. The significance given to these events is seen most of the time in light of the Old Testament. Thus in the piece of the *kerygma* preserved in I Corinthians 15: 3-5, it is said that Christ died, and rose the third day, "according to the Scriptures." And in the further "proclamations of the gospel" found in the book of Acts, the Christ event is seen as the fulfillment of prophecies (Acts 2:16, 23). And so, in this belief, the New Testament writers constantly quote the Old

Testament in reference to Christ and the church. For example, in John 15:25 the author discovers a reference to the persecution of Christ in Psalm 69:4: "they hated me without a cause." In John 2:17 he finds a description of Christ's cleansing of the temple in Psalm 69:9: "zeal for thy house will consume me." In John 19:28 he finds a prophecy of Christ's dying thirst in Psalm 69:21: "I thirst." Yet the whole psalm can hardly refer to Christ in a predictive sense, since there are also statements about sinfulness (69:5), and vindictiveness (69:22-29). Given this New Testament precedent, later Christian writers carried it on in detail to the extreme (cf. R. Grant, *A Short History of the Interpretation of the Bible*).

The modern reader is often hard pressed to justify this New Testament use of the Old, for it all appears to be so contrived. Yet we cannot dismiss the New Testament references simply as an ancient method of interpretation, for the very proclamation of the gospel is tied up with this, as I Corinthians 15 shows. What the New Testament writers meant was that the coming of Christ was the fulfillment or realization of promises and ideals and hopes and experiences found in the Old. Christ is the end of the story of God's work in the world for the redemption of mankind. The first part of the story is found in the Old Testament. There we find the same God at work, with the same purpose, that has been revealed in Jesus Christ, the second part of the story. So the experiences that came to Israel and its people are similar to those which have taken place in the days of Christ and the church; indeed, much of the Old Testament typifies or corresponds to that which occurred in the New.

This is simply because what God was doing with Israel was part of the same program destined and planned to lead to Christ. So in the quotations from Psalm 69 — they hated me without cause, zeal for thy house has consumed, thirst — John was not denying an original reference to the psalmist's own experiences, but rather he was looking over history and saying that Christ summed up all that the psalmist said about the suffering and persecution of the innocent. Christ was the supreme example of someone who suffered unjustified hate, and by his suffering brought in essence the end to suffering. The kind of thing the psalmist suffered is the kind of thing Jesus suffered — unjustified hate in the fulfilling of God's will — because both were part of the plan of God, but at different stages. In other words, the gospel is the final interpretation of God's revelation. All of Jesus' actions — his baptism by the Spirit, his identification of himself with the Servant, his claiming of the title "Son of Man," his participation in a new passover at the Last Supper — show that he understood his work as the fulfillment of the relationship between God and man promised and hoped for in the Old Testament.

C. H. Dodd, in his *According to the Scriptures*, has brought greater understanding of this. He points out that the New Testament writers used certain broad portions of the Old Testament more than others (Isaiah, Jeremiah, Psalms, and a few of the minor prophets) as a special group or body of Scriptures which was recognized as authoritative for explaining the gospel. In other words, Peter said at Pentecost that the events in Christ's life happened "according to the definite plan and foreknowledge of God" (Acts 2:23). But how could this be? In order to show this the New Testament writers continued to quote certain basic passages in the Old as especially indicative of this, because the God who was working in the Old was the same God who was working in Christ. Thus Psalm 69 was not only quoted in the three places mentioned in John, but also 69:9 is cited by Romans 15:3; 69:21 by Matthew 27:34; and 69:25 by Acts 1:20. All this suggests that Psalm 69 belonged to a group of passages which was specially drawn on by the New Testament writers for their exposition of the gospel. Now, however, the New Testament does not use isolated prooftexts out of context, that is, passages or expressions which just coincidentally bore a similarity to incidents in the gospel account, but rather it uses selected verses which point to the teaching of the whole context. The reader was thus invited to study this context, and to reflect upon the "plot" there unfolded. The New Testament writers were interested in the theme of the whole context, and used particular verses to highlight this.

One theme in particular was stressed — the suffering and triumphant servant of the Lord. Thus the New Testament writers drew on a wide range of passages, all of which in context have this same basic plot — Isaiah

52-53; Psalms 8; 22; 31; 34; 69; 80; 118; Daniel 7; Joel 2-3; Zechariah 9-14; Isaiah 6:1—9:6. The plot is that the "hero" suffers shame, ignominy, torment, disaster, and then by the sheer grace of God is delivered, raised up, glorified. The "hero" may be an individual or Israel as a whole, the deliverance may only be promised or hoped for, the reason for suffering may be due to the judgment of God upon sinful people, or to the persecution of an innocent victim, but in all cases the point is the same — humiliation and suffering turned into triumph by the grace of God.

So what the New Testament writers were saying in quoting the Old was that these experiences of suffering and these hopes of triumph have now come to fulfillment in Christ. The "day of the Lord" has arrived, and now all the tragic experiences of the past are made clear. God has had one purpose through it all, namely, that through obedient suffering and gracious triumph the world will be redeemed. The Old Testament experiences of the people of Israel were types or correspondences to the experiences of Christ and the church. What the Old Testament servant experienced (but always with the note of promise for triumph), the New Testament servant experienced (but now in fulfillment). Thus Peter in Acts 2 sees Joel's prophecy of the day of the Lord being fulfilled in his day. So typology is concerned with historical correspondence, not with detailed spiritual truths. The Old Testament hope of a land, a rest, and long life with physical pleasures becomes the hope for eternal salvation in the New. Titus' allusion to the laver (Titus 3:5), Paul's use of the veil (II Cor. 3:7ff.) and of the sin offering (Rom. 8:3), and Hebrews' reference to the altar of burnt offering (Heb. 13:10) are not exact analogies, but rather general historical correspondences with worship elements in old Israel. Therefore it is incorrect procedure to look for parallels in shape or color.

The case for a typological interpretation of the Old Testament seems to be well-established, but there are dangers for contemporary exegesis. *First*, there is the danger inherent in the use of the word "typology," because of the misuse within church history. Contemporary application of typology *is* quite different than the detailed use of the Fathers and others. And in order to avoid confusion many today would prefer the term "correspondence." Secondly, there is the danger that an Old Testament event or figure or institution may be regarded as important only because it provides us with a type looking forward to the New. If this takes place then we miss the meaning and importance that it had in its own context. Revelational significance is not limited solely to its typological content. Thirdly, the application of typology may limit our use of the Old Testament only to those portions where we can determine clear correspondences to the New. But the Old Testament, in large sections, is not typological in this sense. This is true, not only of whole books, such as Ecclesiastes or Job, but also of sections of books where types have been discovered (Exodus, Isaiah), but which also contain many non-typological materials. If these dangers can be kept constantly in view, however, a typological understanding can be of great service in interpretation, for it stresses the unity of Scripture in the ongoing, constant concerns of God which link Old Testament Israel and the New Testament church. The Old Testament then becomes clearly a source book for Christian preaching.

BIBLIOGRAPHY

Dodd, C. H., *According to the Scriptures: The Sub-Structure of New Testament Theology.* New York: Scribner's, 1953.

Grant, R. M., *A Short History of the Interpretation of the Bible,* rev. ed. New York: Macmillan Paperbacks, 1963.

Lampe, G. W. H. and Woollcombe, K. J., *Essays on Typology.* London: SCM, 1957.

Smart, J., *The Interpretation of Scripture.* Philadelphia: Westminster, 1961.

Westermann, C., ed., *Essays on Old Testament Hermeneutics.* Richmond: Knox, 1963.

9

The New Hermeneutic

The new hermeneutic is new in the sense that it departs from traditional hermeneutics. Whereas the traditional hermeneutics was concerned with the detailed principles of interpretation, the new hermeneutic looks upon this as merely a special problem within the much wider activity of interpretation. It is hermeneutic and not hermeneutics because the singular is more carefully derived from the Greek than the plural. Perhaps there is some influence from the German in which the founders of the new hermeneutic write. The Germans use *Hermeneutik* which is a singular.

The literature of the new hermeneutic has been coming into English very slowly but the process has been expedited by the publication in 1964 of *The New Hermeneutic* by James Robinson and John Cobb as volume two in the series, *New Frontiers in Theology*.

The new hermeneutic is a development in continental theology after World War II, emerging from the hermeneutics of Rudolph Bultmann. It is therefore necessary to take a preliminary look at the thought of Bultmann. Bultmann joined with Barth in the 1920's in protest against the methodology of the prevailing religious liberalism. He heralded Barth's *Epistle to the Romans* (1919) as a new breakthrough in Biblical interpretation. Subsequently Bultmann came to the conclusion that Barth was very naive in his appreciation and understanding of critical methods in Biblical interpretation and so he broke with him. Bultmann had been thoroughly trained in critical methodology and his scholarship his entire life long has been characterized by a very critical (if not excessively critical) treatment of the Biblical text.

Bultmann is dedicated to the conviction that science (broadly conceived) and only science can settle matters of fact. This led him to incorporate into his hermeneutics a thoroughgoing anti-supernaturalism. Nothing in the Bible is acceptable that goes contrary to the scientific understanding of things. This obviously excludes miracles but also such supernatural doctrines as the incarnation and the resurrection, and such implicitly supernatural matters as holy history (*Heilsgeschichte*), prophecy, and eschatology. Prophecy involves a view of the divine action which is not acceptable to modern, scientific man. Accordingly Bultmann looks at the Old Testament as a purely human document and as *negatively* preparing the way for Christianity by showing the failure of Israel. It is thus pure law — a position he can readily come by in that as a Lutheran he operates with the law-gospel schema. There is no connected history as such in Scripture or holy history or theology of history; only events of salvation (*Heilstat, Heilsgeschehen, Heilsereignis*).

Furthermore, prescientific and precritical man casts his religious experiences into the form of an external, worldly, historical event. This is, by definition, a myth according to Bultmann. Therefore our hermeneutics demands that the interpreter locate such myths, discard the form that the myth takes because it is prescientific, and yet retain the religious intention of the myth. In this he differs from the liberalism of the nineteenth century which discarded myth and all.

Close attention must be given to the religious intention of the myth. This leads Bultmann to existentialism. According to Franz Theunis (*Offenbarung und Glaube bei Rudolph Bultmann,* 1960), Bultmann had worked out the main lines of his existentialism before he met Heidegger at Marburg but his encounter with Heidegger profoundly influenced his existentialism. There is also direct indebtedness to Kierkegaard in Bultmann. The inner side of religious experience is existential in character (and so in another way he departs from the religious liberalism of the nineteenth century), and therefore the myth is to be peeled off for the purpose of discovering the existential deposit within.

His existentialism in turn leads him to the notion that the Word of God must be address which summons a man to decision either for or against the address. Hence the message of the New Testament as address is kerygma. This in turn must lead to powerful kerygmatic preaching from the sacred desk.

If Bultmann had concentrated on any one of these issues he would have been noted as a typically capable and thorough German scholar. But his creative and dynamic synthesis of all these elements enabled him and and his students to capture the lead in theological scholarship in Germany and Switzerland after the war and so eclipse the neo-Reformed theology of Karl Barth.

The new hermeneutic accepts all of these hermeneutical principles of Bultmann intact. It believes that Bultmann represents the real continuity of the Reformation. That which Luther began with justification by faith they believe Bultmann brings to its fullest development. It is revealing how the new hermeneutic finds so much in Luther and to date has so completely bypassed Calvin. Furthermore, the new hermeneutic believes that Bultmann's hermeneutics represents a historical breakthrough back of which the theologians can never retreat.

But the new hermeneutic is critical of Bultmann on one score. Bultmann did not thoroughly exploit his breakthrough and realize its fuller implications. The precise task of the new hermeneutic is to do this very thing. It has a persuasive defender in Ernst Fuchs of Marburg and a scholar of vast erudition and meticulous scholarship in Gerhard Ebeling of Zurich. Institutes of Hermeneutics have been founded at both Marburg and Zurich. Very little of the writing of Fuchs is in English but there are now two volumes of Ebeling and certainly more to come (*The Nature of Faith*, 1961; *Word and Faith*, 1963).

The new hermeneutic takes as its task the formulation of a theory of interpretation or hermeneutics that is philosophically and theologically more comprehensive than anything heretofor. The older notion of Biblical or Sacred Hermeneutics as well as technical philological hermeneutics among the classicist were far too narrow in their understanding of the issues. Historically speaking, already such men as Schleiermacher and Dilthey had suggested that interpretation was a far more comprehensive task than philologically exegeting texts. This deeper grasp of interpretation was denoted by the German word *Verstehen* which means understanding in contrast to the more superficial and technical explanation (Erklärung) of things. It was the philosopher Martin Heidegger who really grasped this new and far more comprehensive notion of the function of hermeneutics. In his youth Heidegger studied for the priesthood and was introduced to sacred hermeneutics. This stuck within his mind and when he wrote his philosophy in later years he revived it, and, recasting it, gave it a major place in his philosophy.

Taking its clue from Heidegger the new hermeneutic asserts that language itself is interpretation. Language is also profoundly existential in character. Whenever a person speaks he is already engaging in hermeneutics for he is interpreting his world. The word itself is thus hermeneutical and existential. Here a radical shift takes place. Hermeneutics is no longer fundamentally the stating of principles whereby ancient texts are to be understood, but it is a profound investigation of the hermeneutical function of speech as such. Thus traditional hermeneutics functions only in certain special cases and in this respect must be still retained.

Part of the motivation in recasting hermeneutics was to escape the psychologism and historicism of the older critical religious liberalism. In psychologism things are explained exhaustively in psychological terms and in historicism in historical terms of causation and in both instances man never gets out of his skin and is therefore condemned to a vitiating relativism. The new hermeneutic wishes to escape this with its ontological understanding of word.

In reading the literature of the new hermeneutic one is impressed by the flexible use of "word," and grasping its different nuances is one of the more difficult problems in understanding the new hermeneutic. Sometimes "word" seems to mean the existential truth which seeks expression in speech; sometimes it seems to mean the speaking itself; other times it seems to mean the existential depth of the Biblical text; and again at other times it seems to mean the Word of God which breaks out of a sermon. It seems in order for the new hermeneutic to give a breakdown of the different kinds of sentences it uses as the logical positivists once did. Risking such a classification we can note the following kinds of sentences in the new hermeneutic. Some are *programmatic* in that they attempt to state the structure of hermeneutics and understanding as such. Some are *existential* for they seek not to communicate mere information but they intend participation and profound communication. Some are *factual* and *scientific* in that their function is merely to inform whether it be on a popular level ("there is some butter") or on a more theoretical level ("light is composed of rapidly moving photons"). Some are *formal* and only state relationships as in logic, mathematics, or grammar.

In this context of "word" as essentially existential communication the new hermeneutic formulates its concept of the Word of God. The Word of God is really more a movement than a notion. The Word of God is the existential communication of God within the text of Scripture; it is to be dug out by the exegesis and exposition of the text; it is to be formulated in a kerygmatic sermon; and it is received as the Word of God by the hearer when in decision he accepts it by faith. Existential considerations permeate each step of the procedure. For this reason the new hermeneutic is very critical of the so-called neutral, objective, scientific approach to exegesis as represented by Oscar Cullmann. No such exegesis is possible. The expositor must come to his text with existential understanding of religious matters (*Vorverständnis*), but he may not come with a prejudice (*Vorurteil*) as to what the text must say (as in allegorical exegesis).

The new hermeneutic agrees with Bultmann that faith can improperly elaborate its content. The writers of the New Testament had true faith and are our only authoritative witnesses of the Christ event. But as children of their times they were not exempt from error but into their reporting of the Christ event they introduced materials which men of today cannot accept. Although Bultmann stressed myth as that which more than anything else vitiated the reports of the New Testament that is not in accordance with the best of our knowledge, is not binding upon Christians. These foreign materials (foreign to the real existential communication of the Word of God in the texts) are subject to a special form of criticism known as "content criticism" (*Sachkritik*), which is characteristic of the new hermeneutic.

Although Barth does not accept the historic doctrine of inspiration in the Reformed tradition he does believe that once the content (*Sache*) of Scripture is determined it is binding upon Christian conscience. Quite out of step with so much contemporary theology he vigorously defends the existence of angels because he believes the revelation in Scripture commits the Christian to this (*Church Dogmatics*, III/3, p. 369 ff.). Bultmann believes that even if something is the obvious content of the New Testament (e.g., that Jesus rose bodily the third day from the dead) the interpreter is not bound to it. He may believe that this content (*Sache*) is contrary to the scientific understanding of the operation of the universe or the composition of the universe and so reject it as not binding upon Christian conscience. This content criticism came into sharpest focus in the demythologizing controversy, but content criticism in the new hermeneutic is wider than the task of demythologizing (*Entmythologisierung*), and is applicable to all the elements in the New Testament.

The new hermeneutic in extending the work of Bultmann defends a strong kerygmatic interpretation of the New Testament and of Christian preaching. The preacher is to come to the text and pose certain questions to the text. These are not thought of willy-nilly but are prescribed by existential considerations. The text in turn questions the interpreter. Thus in addition to the scientific investigation of the text there must be existential encounter with the text. Only after this is the preacher prepared to preach. Christian preaching must be textual preaching (that is, related to the text of Scripture). Christian preaching is relevant for it is not only shaped by the text, but also by the historical and cultural situation of the congregation. Christian preaching is kerygmatic for it proclaims God's love and forgiveness in Christ, and addresses the listener calling him to the decision of faith.

The new hermeneutic has not been limited to Biblical scholars and theologians but also includes philosophers and other scholars. It is the contention of the new hermeneutic that their understanding of hermeneutics or interpretation is actually the foundation for reconstruction in philosophy, for a new program in epistomology, for a fresh justification of and foundation for the liberal arts, and for a totally new formulation of the nature of Christian theology.

Some of the representative criticisms of the new hermeneutic are: (1) it is still in the liberal tradition in its critical methodology and in looking in the Scripture for the so-called "core" of its meaning; (2) in so restricting its understanding of the supernatural it destroys prophecy and with that any real significance of the Old Testament for the Christian church, and hence is a retreat to the heretical Marcionism of the early church; (3) in so stressing the purely existential and kerygmatic elements in interpretation it eliminates most of the traditional topics of systematic theology and thereby reduces the scope of Christian theology to a very small area; (4) in its notion of faith being pure existential decision it rejects all external props to faith, but only at the price of the ineluctable objective elements in the Christian faith (i.e., it is haunted by the ghost of subjectivism); (5) it has a defective anthropology in that it interprets man in an excessively existential manner and thereby loses the fullness of human nature; and (6) its concept of the Word of God is so opaque or empty (because it is existential communication and not the passing on of mere "information") that it loses real significance.

BIBLIOGRAPHY

Eberling, Gerhard, "Hermeneutik," *Religion in Geschichte und Gegenwart* (third edition), III, 242-262.

——————————, *The Nature of Faith*. Philadelphia: Fortress Press, 1961.

——————————, *Word and Faith*. Philadelphia: Fortress Press, 1963.

Fuchs, Ernst, *Hermeneutik*. Second edition; Bad Cannstatt: R. Muellerschoen, 1958.

Robinson, James M., and John B. Cobb, *The New Hermeneutic. New Frontiers in Theology*, Vol. II. New York: Harper and Row, 1964.

10

Tools of the Interpreter

The saying, "others have labored and you have entered into their labors" is particularly fitting to describe the resources available today to the interpreter of the Bible, resources which represent in many cases lifetimes of work on the part of dedicated scholars. We should not, therefore, apply too strictly the image of tools borrowed from mechanics when we speak of the tools of interpretation. For in the tools for interpreting the Bible, we meet in personal encounter the men who wrote them, and through our entering into their labors we are enabled better to engage the authors of Scripture also in such encounter, and beyond this to encounter the Lord himself who is the true and appropriate subject matter of the Bible.

We assume for the most part in this article that the interpreter is able to handle the original languages; but in case he is not so able, helps and aids are offered here which will assist him no matter what English version he may use as his study Bible. The starting point for all interpretation is, of course, a good critical text of the original languages. The standard for Hebrew is R. Kittel, *Bibla Hebraica* (Stuttgart, 1937), and for New Testament Greek is K. Aland — E. Nestle, *Novum Testamentum Graece* (25th ed.,

Stuttgart, 1963). A good text of the Greek Old Testament (Septuagint) is the one by A. Rahlfs, *Septuaginta* (3rd ed., Stuttgart, 1949). Pastors who depend almost exclusively on English translations should use a fairly literal and modern translation as a study edition and should compare it also with several other modern translations. Frequently, of course, an interpreter may be guided in the text he employs by a commentary written for a specific text. Commentaries frequently offer their own translations.

The primary tools for interpretation are the lexicon, the grammar, and the concordance. These tools should always be at hand, and should be used before the commentary is consulted. Grammatical exegesis precedes theological exegesis. It will be the custom in this article to cite first the most important and useful works in print, and then to refer to other worthwhile volumes. Two works are standard in the field of *Hebrew lexicography*: F. Brown, S. R. Driver, C. A. Briggs, *A Hebrew and English Lexicon of the Old Testament*, edited by G. R. Driver (1906, Oxford, 1952), and *Lexicon in Veteris Testamenti Libris*, by L. Kohler and W. Baumgartner (Grand Rapids, 1951-53). Among lexicons in New Testament Greek, one stands out above all others and has become the standard: *A Greek-English Lexicon of the New Testament and other Early Christian Literature*, translated by W. F. Arndt and F. W. Gingrich (Chicago, 1957) from Walter Bauer's Greek-German dictionary. A more compact lexicon which serves partly also as a concordance, and which lists the Hebrew equivalents for most Greek words is the work by G. Abbott-Smith, *A Manual Greek Lexicon of the New Testament* (3rd ed., Edinburgh, 1937, reprinted 1948). For serious and specialized study in the language of the New Testament, J. H. Moulton and G. Milligan's *Vocabulary of the Greek New Testament* (London, New York, 1914-1930, reprinted 1952) illustrates the New Testament vocabulary from the nonliterary papyri. The two long-popular works on synomyms should also be mentioned here: R. B. Girdlestone, *Synonyms of the Old Testament* (Grand Rapids, 1948), and R. C. Trench, *Synonyms of the New Testament* (Grand Rapids, 1948, reprinted, 1950).

GRAMMARS are normally employed as reference tools by the interpreter, which means that he enters into the riches of the grammar by way of its indexes of Scripture passages and/or Greek or Hebrew words in order to obtain help in unravelling the grammar of his text. However, the interpreter may also find it helpful to study a theme of grammar which has been brought to his attention in preparing a text, or he may study any given aspect of grammar independently of any given text. Both ways of using a grammar should be regularly followed. Some grammars serve one use better than another; and, therefore, the interpreter needs to be acquainted with several kinds of grammars. For Hebrew, the best reference grammar is Gesenius' *Hebrew Grammar* (2nd ed., Oxford, 1910), while S. R. Driver, *A*

Treatise on the Use of the Tenses in Hebrew (Oxford, 1881) is excellent on its subject. The finest and most comprehensive Greek grammar available is F. Blass and A. Debrunner, *A Greek Grammar of the New Testament and Other Early Christian Literature* (Chicago, 1961), translated and edited by R. W. Funk. Another recent and fine work on syntax is Nigel Turner's volume, *Syntax,* Vol. III of J. H. Moulton, *A Grammar of New Testament Greek* (Edinburgh, 1963). The Turner book is more directly applicable to interpretation than the first two volumes of the Moulton grammar. A more concise and summary presentation of Greek grammar is provided by H. E. Dana and J. R. Mantey, *A Manual Grammar of the Greek New Testament* (New York, 1948). This treatment follows the method of the American scholar A. T. Robertson, *A Grammar of the Greek New Testament in the Light of Historical Research* (New York, 1914, reprinted by Broadman Press, Nashville, 1947), which, among other things, employs an eight-case system rather than the usual five-case system. Other grammatical helps worth having on hand are Kenneth S. Wuest, *The Practical Use of the Greek Testament* (Chicago, 1946); C. F. D. Moule, *An Idiom-Book of New Testament Greek* (Cambridge, 1953); and J. Harold Greenlee, *A Concise Exegetical Grammar of New Testament Greek* (Grand Rapids, 1963).

Turning to CONCORDANCES, most pastors will find Schmoller's *Handkonkordanz zum griechischen Neuen Testament* (13th ed. Stuttgart, 1963) designed as a companion volume for Nestle's Greek New Testament, adequate for their needs. One need only know Greek, not German, to use this helpful tool. A more complete Greek concordance, based on the Westcott, Hort and Tischendorf texts, is *A Concordance to the Greek Testament* (2nd ed., New York, 1900) by J. H. Moulton and A. S. Geden. Other Greek concordances available are: *The Englishman's Greek Concordance* (9th ed., London, 1903), compiled by G. V. Wigram, and J. B. Smith, and *Greek-English Concordance* (Scottdale, Pa., 1955). Studies in the Septuagint are greatly facilitated by the excellent and indispensable work by E. Hatch and H. A. Redpath, *A Concordance to the Septuagint and the Other Greek Versions of the Old Testament* (2 vols. and supplement, Oxford, 1897-1906). For Hebrew there is B. Davidson, *Concordance of the Hebrew and Chaldee Scriptures* (rev. ed., London, 1876), which is of more manageable size than the mammoth work of S. Mandelkern, *Veteris Testamenti Concordantiae Hebraicae atque Chaldaicae* (2nd ed., Berlin, 1925). Concordances to English editions of the Bible must now be classified according to the version for which they were compiled. For the King James Version there remain the long standard works by R. Young, *Analytical Concordance to the Bible* (New York, 1879-1894, rev. 1910); J. Strong, *The Exhaustive Concordance of the Bible* (London, 1903), which is indeed exhaustive; and A. Cruden's *Complete Concordance to the Old and New Testaments,* edited by A. Adams, C. H. Irwin and S. A. Waters (Philadelphia, *c.* 1949). Other works for different English versions are: J. W. Gant, *Concordance of the Bible in the Moffatt Translation* (London 1950); M. C. Hazard, *A Complete Concordance to the American Standard Version of the Holy Bible* (New York, 1922); *Nelson's Complete Concordance of the Revised Standard Version of the Bible*, compiled by J. W. Ellison (New York, 1957); and *The Oxford Concise Concordance to the Revised Standard Version of the Holy Bible* (New York, 1962), by Bruce M. and Isobel M. Metzger.

Another indispensable tool is the BIBLE DICTIONARY. Every interpreter should possess a good multivolume Bible dictionary or encyclopedia. They are reference works for historical, geographical, literary, and theological information. An encyclopedia article is often the best introduction to the study of a subject or theme, because its concise form gives an overview of essential points and problems, and in addition usually provides additional bibliographical information. Obviously, all major encyclopedias could be mentioned here, but reference is intentionally limited to works that deserve the title of Bible dictionary; general dictionaries or encyclopedias on religion are omitted. The major dictionaries available are: J. Hastings, *Dictionary of the Bible* (5 vols., Edinburgh, 1898-1904; 12th impression, 1936); *The Interpreter's Dictionary of the Bible*, edited by George Buttrick (4 vols., Nashville, 1962); and the *International Standard Bible Encyclophedia*, edited by James Orr, and revised by M. G. Kyle (5 vols., Grand Rapids, 1930).

Of these, the *Interpreter's Dictionary* is the most modern, but it has not entirely superseded the other dictionaries. The *International Standard* is more conservative theologically. Because they are still available, the two more specialized dictionaries edited by J. Hastings should be mentioned: *Dictionary of the Apostolic Church* (2 vols., Edinburgh, 1915-1918), and the *Dictionary of Christ and the Gospels* (2 vols., Edinburgh, 1906-1908). Many times the interpreter will need the information provided by a Bible dictionary but in briefer form than in the above works. In such cases, a one volume Bible dictionary is a most helpful book to have ready on hand. There are excellent ones available; and they cover a variety of theological positions, although, of course, much of the material in a dictionary does not involve theological interpretations. Among the more recent volumes the following may be recommended: *Dictionary of the Bible* (the one volume Hastings' *Dictionary*, revised and edited by F. C. Grant and H. H. Rowley; New York, 1963); *The New Bible Dictionary*, edited by J. D. Douglas, *et al* (Grand Rapids, 1962); *The Westminster Dictionary of the Bible*, edited by H. S. Gehman (Philadelphia, 1944).

Another tool which belongs with the Bible dictionary and supplements is the BIBLE ATLAS, which is essential for historical and archaeological study and, of course, serves as a useful visual aid in teaching the Bible. Among the better-known and more complete atlases in print are: *The Westminster Historical Atlas to the Bible*, by G. E. Wright and F. V. Filson (Philadelphia, 1945, revised 1956); *Atlas of the Bible,* by L. H. Grollenberg, translated and edited by Joyce M. H. Reid and H. H. Rowley (New York, 1956); *Baker's Bible Atlas,* by Charles F. Pfeiffer, (Grand Rapids, 1961); and the *Oxford Bible Atlas,* edited by H. G. May (London, 1962). A smaller, inexpensive yet excellent atlas is the Hammond atlas, *Atlas of the Bible Lands* (Maplewood, N. J., 1956).

The newest tool for the interpreter of the Bible is the THEOLOGICAL DICTIONARY, or as it is most popularly called, the wordbook. Most simply stated, this kind of book is a theological lexicon; it presents the theological meanings of important Biblical words in terms of their history. Products of the resurgence in Biblical theology, these wordbooks offer a rich and almost inexhaustible treasure of theological knowledge which will enrich the thought and life of the interpreter and help him to make the Word of God luminous. A good wordbook is an indispensable tool; it belongs along with all the other helps such as lexicons and grammars. It is not a substitute for the ordinary lexicon and grammar, but a necessary complement to them. Interpretation always commences with the text of Scripture, not with a tool, good as that tool may be. The most complete and by far the best theological dictionary produced by Biblical scholarship, G. Kittel's *Theologisches Worterbuch zum Neuen Testament,* edited after Kittel's death by G. Friedrich, is now available in an unabridged English translation by G. W. Bromiley entitled *Theological Dic-*

tionary of the New Testament (Grand Rapids, 1964-65). Three volumes are in print; five more are scheduled. This is an expensive set but worth every bit of its cost. This dictionary is based on the Greek text and employs materials from the Old Testament, Judaism, and Hellenism as well as from the New Testament. The dictionary originally was an outgrowth of the work of H. Cremer in his *Biblico-Theological Dictionary of New Testament Greek.* Cremer's book is mentioned here because it is still available from T. & T. Clark, Edinburgh. Kittel's dictionary has spawned a large progeny. The best works only are listed in this article. Two of the most popular and good shorter wordbooks are *A Theological Workbook of the Bible,* edited by Alan Richardson (New York, 1950, also in paperback), and *A Companion to the Bible* (London edition entitled *Vocabulary of the Bible,* 1958) edited by J. J. von Allmen and translated by H. H. Rowley (New York, 1958). *Bible Key Words* (partial translations of some major articles from Kittel, New York, 1949-1964), and *A New Testament Wordbook* (London, 1955) and *More New Testament Words* (London, 1958) by Wm. Barclay are popular, shorter works; *Bible Key Words* is more theological; Barclay's work is more illustrative. Marvin Vincent's long known *Word Studies in the New Testament* (4 vols., New York, 1897-1900), while somewhat useful, does not measure up to the modern theological dictionary and is not a wordbook in the newer sense of the term.

The first help which comes to the mind

of most interpreters when faced with a problem in Biblical study is the COMMENTARY. No one need speak for them; but it is difficult to speak discriminatingly about them because of the vast number of commentaries both new and old which are at the disposal of the interpreter. The other tools mentioned in this article should be used first; the commentary, of course, may be used partially as a lexicon or a grammar or a dictionary or a wordbook. But a commentary is itself a finished product of interpretation. Commentaries come in a bewildering variety of packages: separate monographs on one Biblical book, one volume commentaries on the entire Bible, or on one of the Testaments, and series of commentaries designed to cover the Biblical books one at a time and to employ a more or less uniform method of interpretation. Thus we can speak of critical commentaries, expositional or theological commentaries, and devotional commentaries, depending on which aspect of interpretation predominates over the others. Some famous commentaries, such as Barth's *Epistle to the Romans* (English translation, Oxford, 1933), are more like monuments in the history of interpretation than useful tools for present needs. Nevertheless, the influence of Barth's *Romans* is obvious in many commentaries which have succeeded it. Commentaries are recommended or selected by an interpreter because of the reputation of the author or of a series; most frequently, however, commentaries are bought on personal recommendation. Only some guidelines can be given here. A basic set for the library of an interpreter is *The Expositor's Greek Testament*, edited by Wm. Robertson Nicoll (London, 1910, reprinted Grand Rapids, 1952). One cannot help but mention the multivolume *Interpreter's Bible* (New York, 1951-1957), which is based on a double (KJ and RSV) English text, and which divides the work of exegesis and exposition among the different contributors. This is a dubious method and breaks the unity of scientific exegesis and proclamation which must characterize a proper procedure and purpose in interpretation. The interpreter should not overlook older commentaries. Patristic interpretation is worth consulting for many reasons. The commentaries of Calvin remain models of the art; most of them are still quite usable, and in the case of the New Testament commentaries are available now in new English translation. Luther on Galatians and Romans are musts; but so also is E. D. Burton on Galatians and Sanday and Headlam on Romans in the *International Critical Commentary series* (*I. C. C.*) The Pauline commentaries of Bishop J. B. Lightfoot are excellent; so also is anything by B. F. Westcott, A. Plummer and F. Godet. In the Moffatt commentaries, C. H. Dodd's volumes on Romans and the Johannine letters are very good. In the more recent *New International Commentary on the New Testament*, the volumes by F. F. Bruce (Acts, Colossians, Hebrews), N. Geldenhuys (Luke), F. Grosheide (I Corinthians), and P. E. Hughes (II Corinthians) are noteworthy. William Hendriksen's *New Testament Commentary* (Grand Rapids, 1953) merits notice.

A similar series is commencing for the Old Testament, following a conservative approach. In the new *Cambridge Greek Testament Commentary*, C. E. B. Cranfield on Mark is fine; also C. F. D. Moule on Colossians and Philemon. Other series worthy of attention are the Tyndale series and the *Layman's Bible Commentary*. The interpreter should not overlook the Limited Editions Library of commentaries by Baker Book House. Individual commentaries of note among others would include H. B. Swete on Mark and Revelation; Franz J. Leenhardt on Romans (one of the best); C. K. Barrett on John; Jean Héring on I Corinthians; and E. G. Selwyn on I Peter. In the area of Old Testament commentaries, G. von Rad on Genesis is superb, and A. Weiser on Psalms is excellent.

Several recent editions of one volume Bible commentaries deserve mention. The following three commentaries are in a rough order from middle of the road to quite conservative. *Commentary on the Bible* by A. S. Peake (1919) has been rewritten as *Peake's Bible Commentary*, edited by M. Black and H. H. Rowley (New York, 1962). An evangelical work is *The New Bible Commentary*, edited by Francis Davidson (Grand Rapids, 1953), and a more conservative one is *The Wycliffe Bible Commentary*, edited by C. F. Pfeiffer and E. F. Harrison (Chicago, 1962).

Finally, brief mention may be given to expositions of the Bible which are more sermonic in content than strictly exegetical.

Such works cannot really be classified as tools, but must be considered as helps and secondary ones at that. Their value, if they are used, would be for illustrative purposes, general style and aid in sermonic form; they cannot be the starting point for serious interpretation of the Bible. To be sure, one cannot despise such a work as the *Exposition of the Old and New Testaments* by Matthew Henry (New York, 1708-1710), but Biblical scholarship has moved since then; the tools are sharper; the problems more numerous; yet the possibilities and purposes remain the same, and many of the older devotional helps can remind us, if we need it, why we are interpreting at all.